Supporting Effective Learning

Eileen Carnell and Caroline Lodge

P·C·P

Paul Chapman
Publishing

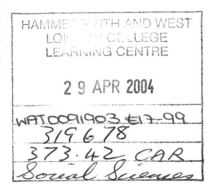
© Eileen Carnell and Caroline Lodge 2002

First published 2002

Apart from any fair dealing for the purposes of research
or private study, or criticism or review, as permitted
under the Copyright, Designs and Patents Act, 1988, this
publication may be reproduced, stored or transmitted in
any form, or by any means, only with the prior
permission in writing of the publishers, or in the case of
reprographic reproduction, in accordance with the terms
of licences issued by the Copyright Licensing Agency.
Inquiries concerning reproduction outside those terms
should be sent to the publishers.

Paul Chapman Publishing
A SAGE Publications Company
6 Bonhill Street
London EC2A 4PU

SAGE Publications Inc
2455 Teller Road
Thousand Oaks, California 91320

SAGE Publications India Pvt Ltd
32, M-Block Market
Greater Kailash - I
New Delhi 110 048

Library of Congress Control Number: 2001132900

A catalogue record for this book is available from the
British Library

ISBN 0 7619 7046 0
ISBN 0 7619 7047 9 (pbk)

Library of Congress catalog record available

Typeset by Dorwyn Ltd, Rowlands Castle, Hants.
Printed in Great Britain by Cromwell Press, Trowbridge,
Wilts.

Contents

Acknowledgements

We would particularly like to thank the following contributors who have provided many of the case studies and examples that illuminate this book:

- Alison Heap, Ethnic Minority Achievement Adviser, Ethnic Minority Central Team (LCAS Development), London Borough of Ealing;
- Patsy Wagner, Educational Psychologist, London Borough of Kensington and Chelsea;
- Sally Wells, Principal of Child and Youth Care Education Service, attached to Boys and Girls Welfare Society, Cheadle, Cheshire;
- Val Dagley, Cromer High School, Cromer, Norfolk;
- Tony Fraser, Helena Romanes School, Essex;
- Lorna Field, Headteacher, Kings Norton Primary School, Birmingham LEA;
- Barbara Patilla, Mulberry School, London Borough of Tower Hamlets;
- Peter Jarvis, Ellen Wilkinson School, London Borough of Ealing;
- Moya Brewer, Access and Development Team (Behaviour Support), London Borough of Harrow;
- Polly McLean.

We would also like to acknowledge the contributions of the many participants at NAPCE workshops and of the MA students in the ALICE Cluster at the Institute of Education, University of London. They extended our thinking on many issues. We would also like to thank the schools in which we carried out research.

We asked many colleagues to comment on chapters in this book. We are grateful to them for the helpful suggestions and comments they made: Gordon Stobart, Alex Moore, Chris Watkins, Val Klenowski, Alison Heap, Sally Wells, Colleen McLaughlin, Tony Fraser, Val Dagley, Sue Askew, Jacqui MacDonald, Barbara Patilla, Sian Williams, Polly McLean, Moya Brewer, Jane Reed and the students on the School Development MA module. We would never have written this book if we had not been part of a team who wrote *Effective Learning* and *Learning about Learning.* Our colleagues were Chris Watkins, Patsy Wagner and Caroline Whalley.

There are others who have supported us in writing this book and to whom we would like to give special thanks: Ann Doyle, Isobel Larkin, Bea Raken, Anna Lodge, Robert Pryce and other members of the AGEL team.

Introduction

This book focuses on young people as learners and how their learning in schools can be supported. Many teachers will have heard statements similar to this comment by a Year 10 student: 'It's not that I haven't learnt much. It's just that I don't really understand what I am doing' (Harris et al., 1995: 253). Many young people share this student's lack of understanding about how they learn, how they learn most effectively, what alternative strategies they could use, what conditions suit them and so forth. The helplessness expressed by the Year 10 pupil is striking. This young person is saying that if they understood more about what they are doing they would learn more effectively. This book argues that helping young people understand more about learning is a key function for teachers, individually or acting collectively, and for others who have a role in supporting their learning.

We want a focus on learning, not to the exclusion of teaching, or indeed of content. We are concerned that a focus on teaching and teachers in UK schools in the last 15 years has distorted the relationship between teaching and learning, by excluding the latter, or by assuming that learning will result from effective teaching, as if the learner and the learner characteristics are irrelevant. We argue in this book that now and in the future we need learners who are expert in learning, because they live and will continue to live in rapidly changing circumstances. Expert learners have developed a capacity to make sense of their experiences of learning, in different contexts and for different purposes.

The purpose of this book is to examine aspects of secondary schools that can contribute to the development of this capacity and so enhance young people's learning. It is a distillation of new knowledge, thinking and experiences, intended for busy teachers.

Our first purpose is to support the shift from teaching to learning. Effective learning requires an explicit focus on learning. To be explicit we need the language to express our ideas. Our vision is to develop a rich learning language through dialogue. Talking about learning extends the learner's capacity to learn. We use a number of different theoretical perspectives to inform teachers' practice. For example, we show a cycle of learning that can be used at a meta-learning level to help make sense of one's experiences of learning. Learning is not easy or straightforward, but complex and multidimensional. The more the learner understands this, the richer their learning will be.

The second purpose is to help learners understand better the importance of context. We discuss how learning is different in different contexts. Learning needs to be made sense of in a variety of contexts, within and across the school and outside school. Through an awareness of their context and its effects, learners are able to have an influence on this context and to understand the differences between contexts. Again we argue that this awareness is essential for learning in the twenty-first century.

Our third purpose is to help those in schools understand the value of creating a learning community and experiment in developing them in their classrooms, tutor groups and in the whole school. In a learning community, the learning of all members is richer than it is in isolation. We promote the idea of all the different layers in the school learning together to reinforce and complement each other's activities – tutor, classroom teacher, pastoral teams and the whole school organization. In this community we see learners occupying different roles, and they have opportunities to learn in reciprocal learning relationships. We look at learning communities at different levels and with different combinations of people.

Our fourth purpose is to help learners make connections. Lives in the twenty-first century are complex, and effective learners are those who make connections with previous learning, other learners and different contexts. We also examine connections in young people's learning, especially between their learning in and outside school and with their parents and others in the community.

Our fifth purpose is about encouraging teachers' learning about learning. If teachers are able to understand themselves as learners they are more able to support the learning of others, both young people and colleagues. From this perspective we address how teachers can enhance young people's learning.

Because our purpose is to encourage a rich, complex and explicit conception of learning among members of the school community, we have not written a how-to-do it manual. In this book you will not read about how to improve your performance or teaching skills and competencies. It is not a book about knowledge, or curriculum subjects or about thinking or study skills for young people. This would not be congruent with our conception of learning. However, a focus on effective learning will undoubtedly help young people and teachers.

We invite our readers to imagine learning schools. What would we notice about people and learning in these schools?

In schools for learning we would notice that:

- Learners are effective – active, responsible, collaborative in their learning, aware of their purposes, feelings, strategies and contexts. They use meta-learning strategies to make sense of their experiences of learning. They embrace complexity and difference in their learning. (See Chapter 1.)

- Classrooms are rich learning environments where learners are flexible, collaborative, resilient, resourceful and reflective. They are engaged in challenging tasks that involve learners in dialogue, in assessing their own learning and in using feedback as part of their learning. The language of learning is developed as part of classroom activity. Students are less dependent on their teachers and hierarchy is less evident. (See Chapter 2.)
- Many people come together to pool their resources to help young people whose learning is at risk. They adopt a holistic approach, taking account of the context in which the young person is living and expect to meet different needs differently. The strategies used to minimize risks to their learning take account of complexity. (See Chapter 3.)
- Tutoring is seen as a key role for supporting learning and the tutor is developing a special position in relation to the students and the context in which they learn. They are helping the tutees to connect their learning across the curriculum and they are developing a programme for learning about learning. (See Chapter 4.) Tutoring for learning through individual learning conversations is structured using the *Do, Review, Learn, Apply* cycle. The focus is on learning targets rather than performance targets. Meta-learning is used to help young people make sense of their experiences of learning. (See Chapter 5.)
- Schools are developing deliberate and explicit connections between parents, teachers and others in the community to support young people's learning in different contexts. Schools' organizational patterns and approaches are changed by these connections. (See Chapter 6.)
- The pastoral teams are developing a special position to support the learning of young people. They look at the whole young person, taking account of their personal, moral, spiritual and academic development. They provide a structure for feedback and guidance for young people's learning. To the wider community they provide a coherent view about young people's experience at school, searching for patterns that promote learning. (See Chapter 7.)
- The teachers use research to encourage rich learning environments for themselves. They take risks, try out new ideas, and involve young people in their research, their responses and views. They talk about their own experiences of learning. (See Chapter 8.)
- The school's relationships, structures and routines support learning at every level. Schools are places where people want to be together, learn together, research together, generate new knowledge together, are excited together and feel powerful together. (See Chapter 9.)

This is our vision, where schools are essentially places of learning, learning which connects to the complexity of young people's lives now and in their futures. These are the schools that our teachers and our young people deserve.

To engage the reader in thinking about rich learning experiences we have drawn on a number of different voices. We include in every chapter a number of examples or case studies to provide illustrations from schools where these ideas are being realized. We have chosen a range of different practitioners with considerable expertise and understanding to offer. They speak from their particular contexts and are often lead learners in their organizations. Many of these practitioners have been involved in research and investigations in their own places of work. They often indicate how they are reflecting on their changing practice. We also include research that draws on what young people themselves say. These young people provide important insights into their experiences of learning, both at school and elsewhere.

We have written this book because of our experiences at the Institute of Education, University of London in an academic group called Assessment, Guidance and Effective Learning (AGEL). The members of this group engage in collaborative learning projects that include research, writing and teaching. We have an explicit focus on learning – our own as well as that of others. It is a rich learning community that stimulated us to think more deeply, take directions in research, read widely, discuss, teach courses and engage with teachers in many different ways about learning. This interaction has helped us to see that the kind of book we would like to refer to did not exist – until now.

We have written the book needed by teachers who want to ensure that schools reclaim the agenda – it is about learning. It is all about learning: teachers and teaching are about learning; schools are about learning; education is about learning; assessment, curriculum, even standards and performance are about learning. Yet, too often schools find they have not contributed to learning and may even have blocked it.

Our separate histories mean that together we have used our experience, all our thinking about learning, the knowledge we have gained as learners and our many connections with learners. Eileen began her career in a comprehensive school in London. As a form tutor and head of year she found great satisfaction in helping individual young people gain access to learning. Later she became involved in an action research project developing Personal, Social and Health Education programmes (PSHE). Other responsibilities include working as an advisory teacher, a director of a teachers' centre and an inspector for professional development and PSHE. Caroline's career began in a rather ad hoc fashion, and continued in this way through almost every post in secondary schools, including tutor, class teacher, head of department, head of year and faculty, deputy headteacher and headteacher. We are now both students and lecturers in education. Among our joint experiences has been running workshops for the National Association for Pastoral Care in Education (NAPCE) and for other organizations. This led us to write materials for teachers' professional development, and then to this book.

We have been through a period when educational experts, the educational establishment and those in schools have been derided and their cumulative and separate knowledge ignored in successive policy initiatives. Most ignored of all have been the young people for whose benefit these policy reforms have been made. Young people are tested more times than ever before. The curriculum has been firmly directed from central government agencies. Young people's achievements are downplayed in order that the media can talk about failure in international tests, pursuing their obsession with failure.

Recent government initiatives have led schools and teachers to focus on performance, intended to do something usually called 'driving up standards'.

It is a distortion to believe performance in tests relates to the quality of learning. Many tests which youngsters undergo have their origin in a concern about school standards, and are used to evaluate the quality of schooling. Caroline's daughter came back from school one day, when she was in Year 9, saying, 'I thought schools existed to help me, but they say I should do well in the SATs tests so that the school can say it is doing well'. A second distortion, then, is that young people are there to serve the interests of schools. This book is for those teachers who want to support young people's learning.

So we find ourselves wishing to write more, to follow up more ideas, projects, case studies and examples. This is not the end. It is our position at the moment. As we go on thinking and talking about learning we realize there is so much more to understand. We would like to continue examining the complexities of learning and to do this with teachers. We would like readers to get in touch with us to continue the dialogue to broaden the discussions we have enjoyed so much in writing this book. We would like you to contact us at c.lodge@ioe.ac.uk and e.carnell@ioe.ac.uk, or through the Institute of Education website www.ioe.ac.uk.

1

The Learner and Learning

Schools exist to promote young people's learning. This book explores how young people can become more effective learners and how schools can promote more effective learning. This chapter focuses on young people as learners and sets the scene for the book by exploring what is meant by learning and by examining some different models of learning. We draw on the fast-expanding field of theory and research into learning to consider how young people can become effective learners.

We introduce some themes that will be developed further throughout the book. We consider which of three models of learning is most likely to promote effective learning. We describe effective learners as active, responsible and collaborative in their learning, and able to reflect on and develop appropriate learning strategies. In order to become effective learners, we argue that learners need to become aware of their purposes, strategies and feelings and of the effects of learning and the contexts of their learning. The most important theme developed throughout this book is that both learners and teachers should be explicit about the ways in which young people are learning, that is, about their learning at a meta-level.

In pursuing these themes we find ourselves confronting the distortions in learning that are produced within schools because of the busyness and complexity of daily life, the tensions that can arise between the need for order and creativity and the current emphasis on performance as a measure of learning. We find ourselves challenging traditional views of learning: for example, that it is a private activity, undertaken individually.

The chapter examines the following aspects of learning:

- conceptions of learning;
- models of learning;
- effective learning and effective learners;
- learners' beliefs;
- learning styles;
- learning relationships.

Conceptions of learning

We begin by noting that the word 'learning' covers a range of different meanings for people. Everyday conceptions about learning include the following:

- getting more knowledge;
- memorizing and reproducing;
- applying facts or procedures;
- understanding;
- seeing something in a different way;
- changing as a person (Marton et al., 1993; Saljo, 1979).

These different conceptions may be held by different people or by the same person in different circumstances and for different purposes. The list begins with a mechanical view of learning: taking in or consuming more information. Learning to recite your 'times tables' is clearly in the second meaning of memorizing and reproducing. Applying those tables to help solve mathematical problems involves the third meaning of applying facts or procedures. The list moves on to include seeing the learning as making meaning, interpreting events and constructing knowledge or understanding. Later in this section we will consider what constructing knowledge means.

We should not overstate the final conception of learning in this list: changing as a person. This refers to a process that is usually gradual. In this sense, changing as a person can refer to cognitive, social or emotional states. A young refugee becomes competent in English and this enables the young person to take an active part in the classroom and social activities alongside their peers. Receiving a small piece of feedback, such as a comment that in a conflict situation they always make a joke, enables the joker to consider whether this is always appropriate and to choose to change their reaction. Another young person considers with awe some aspect of the natural world and is enthused to explore the phenomenon further. Some aspects of their studies have changed the way each of these people look at the world and are changed by it.

These conceptions of learning all relate to what the learner is doing. We can also consider different purposes in learning. A recent United Nations Educational, Scientific, and Cultural Organization (UNESCO) report, *Learning: The Treasure Within* stresses the need for everyone to learn for four different purposes (International Commission on Education for the Twenty First Century [ICE], 1996):

- learning to know;
- learning to do;
- learning to live together;
- learning to be.

The report describes these as the four pillars of education. It argues that people need to learn how to know because in the twenty-first century the volume of evolving knowledge and know-how will continue growing. Watkins et al. (1996) describe the implications of this growth:

- The knowledge base in society is increasing rapidly, and now doubles every four years.
- In a society increasingly organized around the processing of information, more effective learners are required.
- In a learning society, employment prospects relate more to the ability to enhance and transfer learning than to the accumulation of qualifications.
- People need to learn in an increasing range of contexts, not just the compulsory ones (Watkins et al., 1996).

Learning to know

Learning that takes place in school has traditionally been mainly concerned with learning content, but the UNESCO report argues that 'it is not enough to supply each child early in life with a store of knowledge to be drawn on from then on' (ICE, 1996: 85). The volume of information available to everyone continues to grow and its nature is changing. Everyone will need to know how to deal with this unprecedented situation in the future. Acquiring information is not the same as learning how to know. 'Learning to know presupposes learning to learn' (ibid.: 87). Young people need to learn how to find, evaluate, sort, interpret and connect the information available to them.

Learning to do

Learning to do has often been given second-best status and considered more suitable for those thought of as less able, as the history of vocational education in this country demonstrates. It has become less easy to predict what young people will need to learn to do. Learners will find that it is not adequate to respond to changes that have already occurred but that they need to anticipate future needs. This means learning to manage change and diversity and to develop the skills for self-directed learning (Hayes et al., 1995). In vocational as well as other spheres it is no longer a matter of simply acquiring specific skills, rather it is the ability to be flexible and to learn and work with others that is increasingly being required. This has implications for how young people learn in schools, which we consider in Chapter 2.

Learning to live together

Some schools explicitly plan to help young people learn to live together and to equip them to live in an increasingly complex world. The UNESCO report suggests this is 'probably one of the major issues in education today' (ICE, 1996: 91). The impact of technological change upon our social world already means that people need to know how to relate to many more people, in many more roles and using many different media. It can be hard to promote this kind of learning when schools are dominated by the importance of demonstrating that knowledge has been acquired.

Learning to be

The UNESCO report suggests that learning to be, the fourth pillar, is a summation of the other three kinds and is to do with the development of the whole child, a holistic approach to learning. 'In that connection, education must not disregard any aspect of a person's potential: memory, reasoning, aesthetic sense, physical capabilities and communication skills' (ICE, 1996: 97). It argues that these four pillars need attention from early childhood and throughout life so that people are equipped to meet the demands of a complex and changing future.

Many argue, as we do, that a shift is needed from focusing on *teaching* to focusing on *learning* and from *teacher responsibility* to *learner responsibility*. Arguments for different sorts of learning experiences in the future support this shift:

> As we move away from the bureaucratized systems of industrialization to the more fluid insecurities of the twenty first century school learning should be about learning how to learn for self-development in a social world oriented to mutual respect and support rather than competitive individualism tied to individual self-interest and fragmented competencies. (Wallace, 1996: 68)

Others argue for a shift from fragmented competencies to a more holistic approach to learning. Claxton (1999) for example, suggests a new classification of the three Rs: Resilience, Resourcefulness and Reflectiveness. These are connected human qualities and represent a different conception of learners than the traditional 3Rs suggest. Resilience, Resourcefulness and Reflectiveness indicate learner empowerment gained through collaboration, problem-solving, interdependence and a sense of purpose, negotiation and meta-learning (see below). Both Wallace and Claxton argue for a sense of coherence in young people's learning and for learning activities to be based around social interchange.

In this section we have been considering what learning means to young people now and in the future. The themes which will be developed through this book are that learners need to be prepared to become flexible, collaborative, resilient, resourceful, reflective and less dependent upon their teachers. In the future young people need to learn about how to learn, how to learn collaboratively and to pay attention to physical, emotional and social aspects of learning. We now consider some different models of learning and evaluate how likely they are to encourage this kind of learning.

Models of learning

The exploration of meanings of learning in the previous section helps us understand that the word 'learning' is used in many ways. But these perceptions do not help us think about how learning happens. There are different views about this. We now turn to three different models of learning that help us understand how learning occurs:

- reception model;
- constructivist model;
- co-constructivist model.

Reception model

In this model the learner is a passive recipient of knowledge which is transmitted by the teacher, as its name indicates. This model of learning can be linked to the first two of the everyday meanings of learning discussed above: it is concerned with the acquisition of knowledge, and with memorization and reproduction. In this model basic essential skills are emphasized while emotional and social aspects of learning are not addressed. Teaching in this model resembles transmission and stresses cognitive learning and logical, objective, abstract, sequential thinking.

Examples of this model are:

- the National Curriculum – this defines for schoolchildren what they have to take in, regardless of their context, experience, interests or needs;
- GCE O level examinations – the key skills required for success are memorization and reproduction of information. While the 16+ examination system has changed in the UK, many children in other countries still sit GCE O level examinations;
- times tables – when an education minister, Stephen Byers, speaking to the press about the Department for Education and Employment's (DfEE's) numeracy programme in 1998, replied 'fifty four' to the question 'what are seven eights?' it caused an uproar. Educated and responsible people are expected to have learnt their tables.

This model could be described as quantitative, as learners are concerned with how much they can learn. Paulo Freire describes it as the banking concept of education: 'Education thus becomes an act of depositing, in which the students are the depositories and the teacher is the depositor . . . In the banking concept of education, knowledge is a gift bestowed by those who consider themselves knowledgeable upon those whom they consider know nothing, (Freire, 1970: 53).

The learner's role is seen as quite distinct from the teacher's. A problem with this model is that it encourages closed or fixed conceptions of the learner. These conceptions may be held by the student, the teacher and the parents. Often these conceptions refer to ability or intelligence, which we know teachers assess early in their contact with classes, and construe as stable (Cooper and McIntyre, 1996). Many learners also come to define themselves in terms of ability and this can lead to beliefs about *inability* when faced with difficult learning tasks. These beliefs can be reinforced through this model of learning (see below).

This model of learning can also encourage dependency by the learner on the teacher. To continue with Freire's metaphor, it is other people's knowledge that is being deposited, and the learner is not being encouraged to think critically. Morgan and Morris find that pupils believe that teachers' actions are the most powerful determinant of how much they learn (Morgan and Morris, 1999). This research suggests that both teachers and pupils ascribe learning to characteristics found in the other: pupils believe that learning is determined by teachers and teachers believe that it is the pupils' attributes (ability, intelligence, social background and motivation) that determine how much they learn. These problems with relationships in learning are explored later in the chapter.

In the reception model the learner does not define the curriculum and it is not negotiable. The learner merely receives information which others have deemed significant.

Assessment is largely related to the quantity of knowledge learned, and to mastery of basic skills. Feedback is largely a gift from the teacher to the learner, and usually summative (Askew and Lodge, 2000). It is largely evaluative, which does not help the young person learn or improve:

> Sometimes if she just puts B at the bottom and doesn't put corrections – you think, well, what have I got to do to put it right? (Year 10 student, quoted in University of Bristol, 2000).

> Once she said 'you're not very good at spelling.' I don't really want to hear that because I already know that. (Year 10 student, quoted in University of Bristol, 2000).

> 'Not very good work' doesn't help me to know how to do it better. (Year 3 student, quoted in University of Bristol, 2000).

The phrase 'killer feedback' was coined to describe situations when the feedback actually blocks learning by giving unclear messages, by being overpowering or by not giving help in how to make changes. The person giving the feedback does not connect with the learner's purposes (Askew and Lodge, 2000). As one young person said about criticism without guidance, 'It makes you feel sad and doesn't help improve work' (University of Bristol, 2000). This kind of feedback often encourages students to think about themselves rather than the task, as this quotation indicates.

In the previous section we suggest that effective learners are those who have learnt how to know. The reception model of learning does not encourage selectivity and judgement about what it is important to know. It does not encourage transfer of learning to different contexts, and it fails to address the learner's understanding of themselves as a learner. It is likely to encourage a dependence on others to decide what is important rather than develop the ability to learn throughout life. Young people are not encouraged to make connections, apply their knowledge in unforeseen circumstances or see things in different ways. In short, this model does not encourage the kind of learning young people need for their futures. The acquisition of knowledge, its memorization and reproduction are important in learning of learning, but are not enough for learners now or in their futures.

Constructivist model

The term 'constructivist' indicates that the learners' construction of meaning is at the heart of this model. Learners are highly involved in making meaning. They actively construct knowledge through such activities as discussion, discovery learning and open-ended questioning, usually related to their everyday experiences, often with the help of those around them. The emphasis is less on *putting in* information and more on *drawing out* new knowledge and understanding. The emphasis is not so much on the quantity, but more on the quality of the learning. The learner is helped to make connections and to gain new insights.

Examples of this model are:

- formative assessment – feedback comments that focus on helping the learner see and understand what can be done next, or differently;
- research activities – students identify what they need to know and find sources of information to extend their previous knowledge;
- investigative activities that invite students to find their own patterns and relationships.

In this model, the teacher is seen more as a facilitator. The responsibility for learning partly rests with the learner. The learner's ability is not seen as fixed, but capable of development through experience. The teacher is interested in finding out each learner's abilities, skills and interests. The relationship of the teacher to the student, however, remains one of expert to novice.

The curriculum, in this model, emphasizes relevance. Learning situations take account of social and emotional factors, but cognitive development is still the main purpose of learning. The development of the ability to process, acquire and relate information to the learner's own experiences is seen as especially important in this model. Research into teaching strategies that teachers and students find to be particularly powerful identifies group and pair work, storytelling, use of stimuli that relate to student pop cultures, drama and roleplay, use of pictures and other visual stimuli. The researchers comment on the students' preferences: 'A powerful feature uniting all these preferred strategies was the opportunities they all provided for pupils to represent information in ways that they found personally meaningful' (Cooper and McIntyre, 1996: 110). Assessment in this model may rely partly on knowledge recall and interpretation, but can also include presentation of self-selected projects, portfolios, interviews and other less traditional forms of assessment.

Feedback in this model is often described as formative, encouraging further connections and new understanding. It moves from being primarily about judgement to being more descriptive. It has also been described as 'ping-pong', to capture the stimulus and response pattern that it encourages (Askew and Lodge, 2000). This kind of feedback can help the learner understand how to do better or differently:

> I think it's made a difference to my learning, because you get to know what you are supposed to be doing and then how to make it even better. (Year 5 student, quoted in Clarke, S., 2000: 43)

Comments are useful because you get to know how to improve. Like it says there – one too many rhetorical questions. (Sixth form student, quoted in University of Bristol, 2000)

Both these learners refer to the importance of 'getting to know' how to make improvements from feedback comments.

This model of learning encourages some aspects of effective learning. The learner is encouraged to develop their judgement about what it is important to know. It can encourage transfer of learning to different contexts, and may help the learner understand more about being a learner. While encouraging more aspects of effective learning, this model falls short of promoting the kind of learning young people need for their futures. They may remain dependent upon the teachers and not develop those dispositions required for future learners, for example as learners in a team.

Co-constructivist model

The co-constructivist model, as the name suggests, is an expanded version of the constructivist model. The essential features of this model are that it relies on dialogue and that the responsibility for learning shifts from individuals to emphasize collaboration in the construction of knowledge. In this model, learning involves collaboration by learners in critical investigation, analysis, interpretation and reorganization of knowledge, and in reflective processes, in areas that have meaning in the learners' lives. This model of learning takes a holistic model of the learner. It takes into account the emotional aspects of learning, the dynamics of learning with others in groups, the significance of context, the purposes, effects and outcomes of their learning.

Examples of this model of learning in practice include:

- problem-solving dialogue between students;
- dialogues between learners and learners, and learners and teachers that focus on learning; we have in mind tutoring or learning conversations (see Chapter 5).

In a third example, teachers and students were involved in a programme in science classrooms, which aimed for increased learner awareness of the nature and process of learning (Baird, 1986, quoted in Watkins, 2001).

Materials were devised to increase students' awareness and control of their own learning, including a Question-Asking Checklist, an Evaluation Booklet, and a Techniques Workbook. Lessons often included discussions of the purposes of learning, questionnaires about learning, and discussions about the relative roles of teacher and student in learning. After 6 months, 15- and 16-year-olds showed greater understanding of content and more purposeful learning, while the teacher had changed to allow more learner control. (Watkins, 2001: 5–6)

The co-constructivist model of learning is not common in schools, especially where there is an emphasis on performance rather than on learning.

Dialogue is more than conversation, it is the building of learning-centred narrative. Anderson explores the richness of dialogic activities for learning about learning:

> This process encourages learners to be active in their learning and to determine its direction. It makes learning more purposeful and self-directed. It provides opportunities for learners to think about, to expand, to reconsider, to question, and to understand differently. It promotes an opportunity to develop an awareness of and to develop habits of focusing on, thinking about and tracking their learning. (Anderson, 1999: 68)

Thus dialogue prompts reflection, critical investigation, analysis, interpretation and reorganization of knowledge. In this way feedback and reflection become part of the same process, enabling the learner to review their learning in its context and related to previous experiences and understandings. Dialogue also encourages more complex understandings because it is a 'dynamic generative kind of conversation in which there is room for all voices' (Anderson, 1999: 65). We like the words 'dynamic' and 'generative'. They suggest energetic and creative learners who are in control of their learning.

Dialogue has other advantages for learners:

- Unintended outcomes are taken up and developed by the group.
- It makes risk-taking and change less uncomfortable.
- Change invites complex learning. Our fast-changing world is increasing in complexity. We need to help learners develop more complex understandings and handle complexity in their learning.
- It encourages change in the way one sees oneself in relation to others.
- It has the power to transform relationships.

Dialogue is not the same as debate. In debate there is confrontation and a suggestion of winning and losing, whereas dialogue is about building and arriving at a point you would not get to alone. Relationships are important in dialogue, because they must be able to produce the engagement, openness and honesty which dialogue requires.

- Dialogue requires that people be *engaged* in conversation in a spontaneous way, building on the ideas of one another. This is often expressed as excitement, physical proximity, raised energy levels and sudden movements.
- Dialogue suggests people are *open* to new ideas and ways of thinking, new ways of being and not committed to their own point of view. They listen, are tolerant and make new connections. Learners are able to say they have changed their point of view, they are prepared to act differently, that they have made a mistake, or are able to say they are uncertain. They have the capacity to take risks.
- Dialogue requires *honesty*. There is no pretence or side-taking. There is a climate of trust where learners are allowed to experiment with ideas, think things though while talking, and are not afraid if they do not manage to express their ideas quickly or succinctly. Learners take time to explore, to push ideas, and the group is used as a resource.

Each of these qualities – engagement, openness and honesty – is evident in the following observation by a Year 10 student.

> Working in a small group in class is really helpful. You hear everyone's ideas and you can say 'No he doesn't agree with me and why not?' And 'She does', and 'She is sort of halfway'. It is really good because you understand what you think compared with other people's views. (Girl, Year 10, in Carnell, 2000: 52)

The discipline of dialogue involves learning about group processes that support or undermine learning. The ability to communicate effectively about group relationships is essential for co-constructivism. The learning involved in peer dialogue gives learners greater control and responsibility rather than relying on the teacher. Dialogue is grounded in the assumption that learners are teachers and teachers are learners. Hierarchies are broken down and boundaries less evident. The role of the teacher is to instigate a dialogue between and with their students, based on their common experiences, but often the roles of teacher and learner are shared. In this approach learning is seen as complex, multidimensional and involving everyone.

The context, experience and concerns of the participants shape the curriculum. Learners engage in activities or solve problems that have meaning to them so that their learning is intrinsically significant, not just proof that they can do well in school.

In this model assessment and feedback are integrated into the process of learning. Assessment may take many forms, including self or group assessments and include giving an account of the learning process. Feedback in this model has been described as 'loops', to emphasize the way it feeds back into the learning (Askew and Lodge, 2000).

The model of co-constructivist learning has been explored at length for two connected reasons. First, it is not common in schools and, second, it encourages the kind of learning which young people will need for their lives in the twenty-first century. It encourages confidence in dealing with complexity, flexibility and making connections. It encourages people to learn together, and above all it can help learners to become explicit about their learning. There is a need for more of this model in schools, but we do not estimate the forces working against it.

A teacher reading this may respond by saying 'but I include all three of these approaches in my teaching'. This is likely to be the case. We have presented ideal types. This means that they have been created as exemplars in order to discuss their main features and differences. In practice teachers and learners may use more than one model either simultaneously or in sequence.

While teachers might find that pressures from outside the classroom work against these more active approaches, the youngsters themselves largely favour them. A recent study concluded the section on what students have to say about teaching and learning by suggesting that: 'their views concur with what contemporary learning theorists and cognitive scientists have to say about optimal instructional strategies. They prefer an active to a passive role; they prefer transaction to transmission; and they want to learn through a range of activities' (Morgan and Morris, 1999: 66). Further examples of these preferences are given in Chapter 2.

Despite these preferences of the young people, the dominant model in schools remains the reception model, reinforced through the external pressure to cover the curriculum, by teachers' historical role, their view of learners and the cultures of schools. Dialogue flourishes in situations of informality and spontaneity. In this book we suggest that teachers need to see learners as active in the construction and co-construction of their own learning in order to promote more effective learning.

We are not denying that for some purposes it is important that the students perform well in tests and examinations, for example to gain access to a higher level of education or for employment purposes. However, it should be remembered that performance in tests is not the same as learning. We sympathize with teachers who are finding that the pressure to demonstrate improvement can lead them to emphasize the banking concept of education: they need to deposit as much as possible, often referred to as coverage, and their students are under pressure to reproduce this knowledge.

Policy-makers, and others who overemphasize performance, might remember that some learning outcomes may be discernible but that by no means all outcomes are capable of measurement. Moreover, even when we have a concern about performance, we need to remember that a focus on performance can depress performance, whereas a focus on learning can enhance learning *and* performance (Dweck, 2000). For example, we know that giving grades as feedback can undermine motivation and that preoccupation with grades can lead to poorer performances (Black and Wiliam, 1998). The importance of 'doing one's best' was one Year 7 girl's explanation for getting on well with her learning. She said, 'I think positively. I really push myself. I always try my best'. For her, striving to fulfil one's potential – expressed as 'trying one's best' – seemed more important than setting targets. Another Year 7 student, Annie, described her approach to performing in tests.

> Q: Do you set quite high standards for yourself?
> Annie: I just say – do my best – without setting any standard, because I think if I set a standard and I don't reach it then I'm going to be disappointed, but if you do your best and know you've done your best it's okay. (Lodge, 1997: 6)

We note that these two students were speaking about their feelings about doing well, rather than any external assessment of their performance.

In a review of research entitled *Learning about Learning Enhances Performance*, Watkins suggests four ways of being explicit about learning to help learning impact upon performance:

- making learning an object of attention;
- making learning an object of conversation;
- making learning an object of reflection;
- making learning an object of learning (Watkins, 2001).

In this section we have continued to elaborate our theme of making learning more explicit, more visible and more the focus of discussion. In the next section we explore effective learning and its relationship to explicitness about learning processes.

Effective learning and effective learners

Effective learning involves outcomes such as those listed below:

- deepened knowledge;
- higher-order skills, strategies and approaches;
- action towards greater complexity and more learning;
- positive emotions, excitement, enthusiasm;
- enhanced sense of self;
- more sense of connection with others;
- further learning strategies;
- greater affiliation to learning;
- personal significance and change (Watkins et al., 1996).

These outcomes are necessary for people to remain active learners throughout their lives in the twenty-first century. These outcomes will enable learners to approach new and unfamiliar situations and challenges with confidence and excitement.

To encourage effective learning and to promote these outcomes, schools need to develop learners' capacities in four aspects of their learning:

- active learning;
- collaborative learning;
- responsibility for their learning;
- meta-learning.

Meta-learning is a phrase which means standing back from the content of the learning and evaluating the effectiveness of the processes involved – learning about learning. Effective learners are particularly aware of the importance and progress in the following aspects of their learning:

- their purposes;
- their strategies;
- the emotional, social and physical context;
- the effects of their learning;
- the outcomes of their learning.

These aspects of learning are discussed further in Chapter 4, when we consider how the tutor can help the learning of their tutor groups, and in considering how in and out of school learning can be connected across the boundaries of the school (Chapter 6). The ability to stand back from their own learning and monitor what they are doing gives more power to the learner because they can then see how they can change their strategies, find additional resources, and use their energies more efficiently, seek other outcomes or effects and so on.

Young people can develop a capacity to monitor and reflect on the processes of learning through dialogue with others and by using reflective learning diaries or logs. We consider the value of dialogue for becoming conscious of learning processes earlier. In the reflective diaries young people can focus on a particular lesson or task, connections between different activities, reactions to feedback, comments about changes to learning and so on (Watkins et al., 2000). We have read of children as young as 10 years old who have used such logs successfully, one engaging their teacher in dialogue through their log by saying 'these log entries help me a lot. As I write I notice and understand more too' (Sandford, 1988, quoted in Watkins, 2001).

This book is especially concerned with examining ways that schools and teachers can promote these four important aspects of learning: active, collaborative and responsible learning and, especially, meta-learning, that is, learning about learning. In Figure 1.1 we present a cycle of learning that we have found useful in thinking about learning because it describes a cycle of activity, review, learning and further planning.

We have found the focus on reflection and evaluation (Review), the extraction of meaning from this review (Learn) and the planned use of learning in future action (Apply) and further activity in learning (Do) particularly useful. This cycle is useful for focusing on the *content* of the learning, on what was learned.

To promote meta-learning it is necessary to think of two connected cycles, see Figure 1.2. One cycle refers to the content of what is being learned, and the outer cycle refers to the *processes* of learning undertaken. We refer to this as meta-learning.

In this second cycle the same processes of activity, review, learning and application are repeated, but the purpose here is to make explicit and monitor the activities involved in learning the content. We find these cycles of learning very helpful and refer to them in subsequent chapters of this book.

The model that best encourages effective learning and these outcomes is the co-constructivist model. This is because it involves active and collaborative

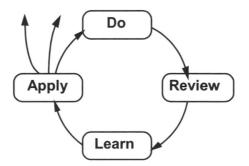

Figure 1.1   *A learning cycle (Dennison and Kirk, 1990)*

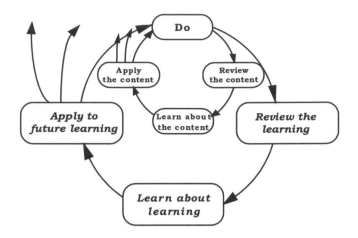

Figure 1.2   *A meta-learning cycle (Watkins, 2001).*

engagement, and is more likely to result in learning that embraces more complexity, and not merely the less rich forms of learning. The desired outcomes are unlikely to result from a reception model of learning. We have argued that all three models of learning (reception, constructivist, co-constructivist) have their place, but current policy and practice tends to restrict learning approaches in schools and discourage the use of constructivism and of co-constructivism. We also argue that there is more scope than might be apparent to develop more of these two models within the school (see Chapter 2).

Learners' beliefs

Teachers reading this book may feel that many young people do not believe that they can learn more effectively. Perhaps the young people believe they are stupid, or have limited ability. Their teachers may see them as having little motivation. We have noticed that teachers tend to talk about the *quantity* of young people's motivation. They talk about needing to increase it, or that there is a problem when young people do not have much motivation. In contrast, when speaking of adults people tend to talk about the *quality* of motivation, saying for example that teachers would be better motivated if they were given more respect.

When young people believe that they need more motivation, they are often puzzled about how to obtain it. Motivation is connected to young people's beliefs, to their purposes in learning, to the context in which they are learning and to the effects of their learning. Focusing on these aspects of learning, as we suggest throughout this book, will help young people understand more about their motivation and help them understand how to approach learning situations to get the best out of them.

Learners' beliefs are very powerful in their learning. The American researcher, Carol Dweck, has used the phrase 'self theories' to describe what we say in our heads about ourselves as learners (Dweck, 2000). What we say to ourselves is based on our beliefs. Her research suggests that most people respond to learning tasks in one of two ways, depending on their context, social and personal factors and other variables. One group holds beliefs which support a mastery orientation to learning: this means they have a love of learning, seek challenges, value effort and persist in the face of obstacles. We call this a *learning* orientation. The other group holds beliefs that prevent them from learning, especially in challenging situations because they link lack of success to lack of ability. We call this a *performance* orientation. The beliefs are summarized in Table 1.1.

Table 1.1 *Learning and performance orientations*

Learning orientation	Performance orientation
Belief that effort leads to success	Belief that ability leads to success
Belief in one's ability to improve and learn	Concern to be judged as able, to perform
Preference for challenging tasks	Satisfaction from doing better than others
Satisfaction from success at difficult tasks	Emphasis on competition and public evaluation
Problem-solving and self-instruction when engaged in tasks	Helplessness: negative self-evaluation when task is difficult

Source: Watkins et al., 1996

Here is a boy who holds a performance orientation: 'In every lesson I work with others but I get a better grade. I want a better grade than the persons I work with' (Year 8 boy, quoted in Carnell, 2000: 53). People are not fixed in all circumstances in these groupings, but because they are founded on learners' beliefs about learning and about themselves they need to be challenged if they are to move from a performance to a learning orientation. People who say 'I am no good with numbers' or 'I can't improve my gym skills because I have two left feet' or 'I never got on with formal, book learning' provide other examples of this negative pattern. One teacher we know described his love of singing as a small boy but he was told to mime at the school concert. He has not sung in public since, believing that he cannot sing as a result of his teacher's concern with performance. When people come to believe that they are unable, or no good at certain things, it is this belief that prevents them from learning, rather than any other reason, according to Freire (1970).

People need to be helped to become aware of their own self-theories so that they can change their understanding about ability and the importance of effort if they hold performance orientation beliefs. Dweck has demonstrated that people can develop a learning orientation, especially when they experience it for themselves and so develop more effective skills. This awareness can be developed through meta-learning opportunities such as are described in Chapters 2 and 4.

Learning styles

Recently there has been an increased interest among teachers in learners' styles. By styles we mean the way in which the learner prefers to learn, the techniques, strategies and preferred activities. There are some techniques for identifying a learner's profile of styles (see, for example, Watkins et al., 2000). These determine the learner's profile in relation to preferences for activity, theory, pragmatism and reflection. We have even heard of schools who experimented with grouping students by preferred learning styles. Those familiar with accelerated learning will be familiar with the trio of initials VKA, which relate to preferences for visual, auditory or kinaesthetic approaches to learning (Smith, 1996). Many teachers find Gardner's theory of multiple intelligences to be very attractive because it recognizes the importance to learning of a range of intelligences, including the highly valued linguistic and logical, but also the interpersonal, the musical and so forth (Gardner, 1983).

Another set of descriptions was developed originally for adults, but has also been applied to young people: active, theorist, pragmatist and reflective learning styles (Honey and Mumford, 1986). These descriptions remind us that people do respond in different ways in different contexts and they can be useful as a checklist to ensure that a range of approaches are included in learning activities. However, we also believe that a word of warning is required. Young people may become labelled, or they may label themselves, as a particular kind of learner: audio-kinaesthetic or activist for example. But styles of learning are not fixed, being highly dependent on circumstance, purpose, conditions, what is to be learned, learner autonomy and so forth. As they are not fixed, the learner can change their styles. In taking styles into account it should be remembered that the styles which have been identified as active, theorist, pragmatist and reflective relate to a learning cycle (similar to the one we referred to in Figure 1.1). This is Kolb's experiential cycle of learning (Kolb, 1984). In describing this cycle, Kolb argued that all four aspects are important, and learners need to engage in all four activities to be learning effectively. It follows that learners therefore need to develop capacities in each of these areas, and experience learning which embraces all four styles.

Young people themselves can see the limitations of too much emphasis on learning styles or a simplified use of the concept. These Year 10 students could see no point in being asked whether their styles were visual, auditory or kinaesthetic:

> Girl 1: When they ask you about what style of learning you prefer – do you like to listen better or do you learn visually – you don't think about that every day. You don't think when you are in an English lesson oh I'm listening, auditory [another says – that's how I learn] and then you are expected to just tell the teacher Oh, I learn by listening and you don't know, you don't think about it.
> Boy: It's like a music lesson; you're going to listen aren't you?
> Girl 2: Or if you're given a film to watch in English you're going to watch it aren't you?

Boy: You're not going to listen to the numbers in a maths lesson.
[laughter]
Girl 1: What are the numbers trying to tell me? (Lodge, 2001)

These young people had understood the need to develop a range of approaches, because they appreciated that this was required by the variety of learning experiences they encounter.

Learning relationships

Another theme referred to throughout this book is to do with positive relationships in learning. Learning is best promoted in a context of trust, respect, and confidence. Pressure and high expectations can be damaging. This Year 10 student was under pressure to perform well and found it very uncomfortable:

> Girl: My teacher frightened me to death because I'd got all top marks, As and stuff and he was going on about how it was expected that I would get all As and A stars in my GCSEs and he was saying, you know, we'll all be disappointed if you don't get that kind of mark. And it was really frightening. And my Dad, 'cos he's kind of like that as well, it was because my teacher had said it he expected it of me and it just frightened me to death – [inaudible]
> Q: So it's not made you feel good?
> Girl: No. I mean it did please me that I got good marks and everything but because now I know that's what is expected if I don't get it I'll be really ashamed of myself. (Lodge, 2001)

This young person was reacting to an emphasis on her performance by significant people who affect her learning.

In later chapters we highlight how the school can promote adults in roles to support learning. Some of these adults are located within the school, such as class teachers, tutors, the pastoral team; others may be based outside the school, but may still influence the learning in significant ways: parents, other family members and connections, the community.

Young people recognize the value of good relationships with adults for effective learning. In their interviews with over 300 secondary students in South Wales, Morgan and Morris found that pupils saw good learning as overwhelmingly derived from the actions of the teachers, and that good relationships with the teacher was an important element in this (Morgan and Morris, 1999). We have noted that young people are often dependent on adults, especially teachers.

This observation is supported by our research with one group of Year 10 students. They valued teachers who responded to the particular class, taking account of their profile of needs. They valued teachers who make an extra effort, like making themselves available to help a young person. They identified three kinds of teachers: those who just do a job, those who are enthusiastic and enjoy passing on their knowledge of their subject, and a third group who live for teaching.

Q: What makes a good teacher then?

Boy 1: Someone that appreciates the students and their efforts in trying to learn, that understands their way of thinking and tries to adapt to that. If they just think – no I'm just teaching this I'm just going to say this and that they don't really care. The ones –

Girl 1: – the ones that think about a particular class and –

Boy 1: Mr S, he thinks – right you should be getting this grade—and he makes the extra effort to make sure you get that grade.

Boy 2: Some of them really care about what you're doing.

Girl 2: Some of them get notes off last year and they say – yeah, we taught this with Year 11 last year and you should do the same as them. And it's somebody who writes personal notes for each student –

Girl 1: – yeah like Mr S. He was telling me the other day about test results. He was saying – I'm always here, hours after school and if you don't understand come and see me because that's pretty much why we're here: to teach you.

Boy 1: Some teachers do the job because they think – it's the job I have to do. They see it as a task. When it's finished that's the end of it. Some teachers, they want to pass their knowledge on and they enjoy that and some teachers –

Girl 1: – like Mr S. I get the impression that teaching is his life.

Boy 1: Someone who makes that extra effort.

Girl 1: Some of them were marking A level papers on New Year's Eve. (Lodge, 2001)

In this discussion the young people are very sensitive to the behaviours of their teachers, but they also see the teachers as responsible for their learning. They are seeing learning as very much within our first two models of learning: the transmission–reception and constructivist model. In the co-constructivist model, learning relationships are less hierarchical and less differentiated.

Of course, young people have learning relationships with each other. Some relationships can be unsupportive: the 'anti-boff' cultures that disparage learning, relationships characterized by bullying, racism, sexism, homophobia and other power relationships. As one young person suggests, some relationships can be especially supportive of learning: 'With friends you don't hesitate, you can say whatever you want – things that just come out of your mouth' (Year 11 boy, quoted in Carnell, 2000: 52).

Establishing effective learning relationships is a key function for schools, and has wider significance for human relations in the future. As we mentioned earlier, UNESCO described this as one of the major issues in education today.

Conclusion

In this chapter we have considered a range of factors which affect the learning of young people, many of which are capable of development by the young people themselves, with support. We have commented on the importance of promoting the capacity of learners to learn more about their strategies, approaches, styles and contexts of their learning. This book makes the case that adults can help young people with this by paying explicit attention to aspects of meta-learning. They can help young people build cycles of action, reflection, extraction of meaning and revising their plans. We will return to the theme of the effective learner, a learner who is active, takes responsibility for their learning, engages with others to collaborate in learning and who engages in meta-learning processes. Each of the chapters which follow consider how different features of the school can promote the development of effective young learners.

Further reading

Askew, S. (ed.) (2000) *Feedback for Learning.* London: Routledge Falmer.

Askew, S. and Carnell, E. (1998) *Transforming Learning: Individual and Global Change.* London: Routledge.

Biggs, J.B. and Moore P.J. (1993) *The Process of Learning.* Englewood Cliffs, NJ: Prentice-Hall.

Watkins, C., Carnell, E., Lodge, C. and Whalley, C. (1996) *Effective Learning.* School Improvement Network Research Matters No 5. London: University of London, Institute of Education.

2

Learning in the Classroom

This chapter develops the ideas presented in Chapter 1 by examining the learner and learning in the context of classrooms. Our purpose is to examine classrooms as learning environments and how conceptions of learning and external constraints affect what happens in them.

We draw on our own and others' research to demonstrate how some classrooms are more effective in supporting learning than others. We make a distinction between the classroom as a context for learning and the role of the teacher in promoting learning-centred classrooms. We look at classrooms as a context for learning and the teachers' role separately in order to understand these distinct concepts and how one might impact on the other. The chapter examines how all classrooms can become rich learning environments and does not relate the ideas to a particular positional role, for example a subject teacher or form tutor.

The chapter focuses on four areas:

- the classroom as a place to learn;
- classroom learning for the twenty-first century;
- factors promoting a rich learning environment;
- factors inhibiting a rich learning environment.

The classroom as a place to learn

What goes on in classrooms is extremely complex. This complexity is analysed by Doyle (1986) who talks of classrooms in terms of their multidimensionality, simultaneity, immediacy, unpredictability, publicness and history. These themes are developed by Watkins (1995) and summarized in Table 2.1.

There are important implications arising from these features:

- Teachers' and students' choices are never simple.
- Teachers and students must monitor and regulate several activities at once.
- Teachers and students have little time, in the main, to reflect before acting.

Table 2.1   *Understanding the classroom context and its properties*

Classrooms are busy places:

- Teachers can be engaged in 1,000 interactions a day; events and decisions happen quickly.
- Pupils receive small amounts of individual teacher attention that is likely to be interrupted.
- Pupils develop skills in coping with interruptions and in learning to wait and learning with peers.

Classrooms are public places:

- Teachers' and pupils' behaviours are visible; teachers may feel on stage.
- Pupils develop skills of getting used to being one of many; they are treated as one of a group not always of their choosing.
- Public evaluations of pupils are given every few minutes.
- Many members of the public take a view on classrooms; teachers may experience role strain and cope by isolating their performance.

Classroom events are multidimensional:

- People in classrooms have a variety of purposes, experiences, interests and goals.
- Personal-social aspects of pupils and teachers are always affecting classroom life.
- Teaching and learning are but one dimension, the formally appointed one.
- When pupils engage in academic learning they exercise considerable skill in focusing on one dimension while selecting out others.

Classroom events are simultaneous:

- Teachers monitor more than they can report (teachers have eyes in the back of their heads).
- The multiple events on many dimensions do not occur in a step-by-step fashion; pupils may use this fact to achieve other goals of their own.

Classroom events are unpredictable:

- No one can predict classroom events with full accuracy.
- Disruptive effects are easily generated by interruptions.
- Yet teachers attempt to predict pupils' responses to learning, pacing of learning.
- Routines attempt to engender predictability and reduce ambiguity.

Source: Watkins, 1995

- Detailed long-term planning is not appropriate and even short-term plans need to be very flexible.
- What teachers do may have important repercussions.
- Planning and decision-making need to take account of a class's history (Doyle, 1986; McIntyre, 1999; Watkins, 1995).

In discussions about the classroom there may be an overemphasis on the teacher and the teacher's responsibilities (Watkins, 1995). This overemphasis has resulted in a focus on teaching rather than learning and behaviour management rather than learning management. These two emphases – teaching and behaviour management – place a particular stress on the teacher's responsibility for controlling events rather than the young people being responsible for their learning. This overemphasis may result in the view that the classroom is the teacher's territory and that young people are guests of the teacher; the classroom is not theirs: 'Classrooms are teachers' territory within which pupils engage with learning on teachers' terms. Those terms change as pupils progress from year 7 to year 11 through an institutionised process of learning upon which pupils have only a marginal influence. The broad agenda is already set' (Wallace, 1996: 59).

Perhaps in primary schools where young people and their teachers learn together throughout the whole day there may be more of a sense of shared space. But in secondary schools young people learn in many different classrooms in the course of one day. They may encounter a number of different classroom routines, management features, layouts, as well as different learning approaches and expectations. All these different aspects will have an effect on their learning and an effect on what kind of learners they become.

Classroom learning for the twenty-first century

When the teacher and young people enter the classroom they all have a set of expectations about what they think is likely to happen and what their role is.

These expectations are very strongly linked with conceptions of learning, and these conceptions influence how teachers and learners go about their learning. Teachers and young people need to enter classrooms with the expectations that learners will be flexible, collaborative, resilient, resourceful, reflective and less dependent on their teachers. In Chapter 1 we describe different everyday conceptions of learning:

- increasing one's knowledge;
- memorizing and reproducing;
- applying, general rules to particulars;
- understanding, making sense;
- seeing something in a different way;
- changing as a person (Marton et al., 1993).

Watkins (2001) warns against describing these conceptions in polarized ways – quantitative versus qualitative, or surface versus deep. He prefers to view them as varying on a continuum from *thin* conceptions to *rich* conceptions of learning.

Classrooms for the twenty-first century need to promote richer conceptions of learning. The everyday conceptions of learning identified by Marton et al. (1993) link with the reception model of learning (see Chapter 1), for example, increasing knowledge, memorizing and reproducing. Other conceptions in this list indicate constructivist characteristics in which learners are making meaning for themselves, for example, understanding and seeing something in a different way. None of these conceptions are necessarily co-constructivist learning conceptions (see Chapter 1). The co-constructivist learning model is not part of everyday talk. If it were, learning conceptions might include generating new knowledge or testing claims, and might refer to associated concepts such as dialogue, relational responsibility and collaborative learning (see Chapter 1). Co-constructivist learning is a richer conception of learning, and by extending the language associated with co-constructivism learners develop richer conceptions of learning.

Dominant in secondary classrooms is the reception model of learning and the dominant language used may not relate explicitly to learning at all but to 'work', 'task completion', 'achievement' or 'performance'. A shift is needed for classrooms of the future to focus on a *learning language*. This would result in richer conceptions of learning.

In examining over 100 research studies in *Learning about Learning Enhances Performance* Watkins reveals important findings:

> Illuminative studies show an association between those learners who hold a rich conception of learning and those who perform well in various learning tasks. But the context has its effect, sometimes because it promotes the association, and other times because it does not (e.g. when rich conceptions of learning are not encouraged in schools).
>
> Intervention studies show the impact of a new strategy for promoting learning, but here again the context is important, not only for supporting the new strategies being tried, but also for embedding them into the complexity of the classroom. There is no single simple intervention with powerful results, so various interventions may be seen as contributions to building a rich learning environment (and in the process grappling with all the contextual pressures which can work against this goal). (Watkins, 2001: ?)

These findings underscore the important effects of the classroom context for learning. Classroom experiences for the twenty-first century need to:

- encourage rich conceptions of learning;
- support new and various strategies for promoting learning;
- resist pressures that inhibit the development of a rich learning environment.

This chapter addresses these issues.

Factors promoting a rich learning environment

This section focuses on:

- a case study;
- strategies for promoting a rich learning environment in the classroom;
- a community of learners;

- collaborative learning;
- activity in learning;
- responsibility for learning;
- meta-learning.

We first examine a case study of a classroom setting where a teacher is experimenting with a group of young people to develop precisely the kind of experiences that promote rich learning experiences.

Case study   *'Learning electronics: an accessible introduction'*

Mike Forret was involved in creating a series of videos on technology for the New Zealand Ministry of Education, and a small group of fourteen year old boys, who had studied an introductory unit on electronics, volunteered to be filmed. They grappled with a problem over the course of a day and a half – an eternity, in school terms, to spend on a single topic. The boys, all unexceptional students, chose a tough problem: designing an electric circuit to turn on house lights when the front door is opened at night (but not during the day), and to leave them on when the door is closed, until turned off at a switch.

After working on this really hard problem that they had chosen themselves, gradually through trial and error and a lot of conversation and argument, they created a satisfactory solution.

When asked what they thought they had got out of this learning experience, the boys said: perseverance; creating a problem you couldn't work out and actually working through and solving it without any help from the teacher. No one knowing the answer was a good feature.

The boys were asked how this experience reflected what else they did in school. They answered:

'We do nothing like this at all in any other subjects, nothing of this calibre. It's all watered down stuff.'
   'Watered down?'
   'It's nothing hard; it's like . . . it may take you twenty minutes to half an hour – everything is aimed to be solved in half a period.'

Forret suggests that students are so used to going through the motions of learning, knowing that there is a standard solution which the teacher is holding back now but will eventually deliver, that quite a different quality of engagement emerges when this is not the case.

It was found that students develop persistence and resilience if given sufficient time to work, preferably in small groups, on a genuinely difficult problem which they have chosen and to which, very importantly, the teacher does not know the answer.

Source: Forret, 1998, cited in Claxton, 1999: 283–4

We now analyse the factors that make this a rich learning experience.

Perhaps the most striking point is that the student activity in the case study is linked with the knowledge gained in activity of day-to-day experience (Barnes, 1986). Learning is happening because learners are doing something for themselves; they are participating, taking initiative, arguing and challenging (Salmon, 1998). Here learning is self-paced, self-directed and non-linear. The situation is less formal than the boys' other classroom experiences. Some argue such informal, contextualized environments are more relevant to the needs of today's learners (Gardner, 1991). The best teaching strategies for engaging students are ones which make 'clear links with the outside world' and focus on 'contemporary events of interest and meaning to students' (Wehlage et al., 1989: 177). (See Chapter 6.)

Learning in this case study is:

- contextualized – the problem is related to real life;
- first hand – the learners have hands-on experience;
- co-operative – the youngsters learn collaboratively to solve the problem;
- self-assessed – the boys review their own learning;
- less structured – the learners are less boundaried by time constraints.

These five categories are used by Resnick (1987) to describe how learning might be characterized if it were out of school. In comparison classroom learning is usually:

- decontextualized;
- second-hand; may need motivating;
- individualistic;
- assessed by others;
- structured formally.

Learning for the twenty-first century needs to be more like out-of-school activity which pupils generally find 'more memorable, more engaging and more meaningful than the more usual classroom based activities' (Wallace, 1996: 59).

The boys were gripped by a genuine challenge that they had created and adopted for themselves. They learned a lot about electronics 'as well as practising some important real-life learning skills'. They also 'articulate and reflect on their own learning processes' (Claxton, 1999: 283–4). Claxton's observations are important because they highlight the fact that activity alone is not sufficient in making learning effective. The stages in the learning cycle, that we introduced in Chapter 1, demonstrate that reviewing, learning and applying also need to be part of an effective learning experience (see Figure 2.1).

This cycle demonstrates that learning needs to be made explicit. In the case study the boys were encouraged to reflect on their learning. They were asked to be explicit about what they had got out of this learning experience. They analysed the process and identified what was helping their learning. They said one of the important elements was not getting the answer from the teacher. They recognized that no one knowing the answer was good. This ability to notice and monitor aspects that enhance learning is essential for effective learning. This highlights the role of self-assessment to enrich learning.

In the case study collaborative activity includes peer discussion, collective discovery, negotiation and joint decision-making. This was a gradual process

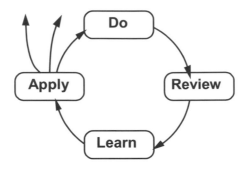

Figure 2.1   *A learning cycle* (Dennison and Kirk, 1990)

of 'trial and error', 'a lot of conversation and argument' and the creation of 'a satisfactory solution'. These are examples of collaborative activity but activity in itself does not necessarily mean collaborative learning.

We make this distinction between collaborative activity and collaborative learning because collaborative activity may remain at the 'Do' stage of the learning cycle (see Figure 2.1). Collaborative learning necessitates an explicit focus on the three other stages – Review, Learn and Apply. In the case study, Mike Forret asked the boys to reflect on the activity and identify their learning. They moved through the cycle. But we do not know whether the boys were able to say in what way they might use the insights gained about their learning on future occasions. We do not know if the learning cycle was completed either by the group or by individuals.

The boys chose a very challenging task. They welcomed high-complexity learning, that is, learning that requires reflection, analysis, judgement, dialogue and collaborative responsibility for learning. Classroom and school constraints may result in an underestimation of learners' capabilities, and tasks set may be too easy, straightforward or fit neatly into the prescribed amount of time. Such experiences may be of low complexity, that is, they are short term, focus on content or skills and do not require judgement. When given responsibility for their own learning these young people set 'high calibre' tasks, not 'watered down' experiences.

Strategies for promoting a rich learning environment in the classroom

The approach taken by the teacher in the case study has much in common with the principles underpinning the 12 strategies offered by Brookes and Brookes (1993) for becoming a constructivist teacher (see Table 2.2).

These constructivist strategies are designed to help young people construct meaning for themselves. Co-constructivism is an extension of constructivism. Co-constructivism can be described as 'learning by being part of a knowledge generating community' as opposed to 'learning by being shown' (imitation), 'learning by being told' (reception) or 'learning by constructing meaning' (constructivism) (Bruner, 1996).

Table 2.2 *Strategies for becoming a constructivist teacher*

- Encourage and accept student autonomy and initiative.

- Use raw data and primary sources, along with manipulative, interactive and physical materials.

- When framing tasks use cognitive terminology such as classify, analyse, predict, and create.

- Allow student responses to drive the lessons, shift instructional strategies, and alter content.

- Inquire about students' understandings of concepts before sharing own understanding of those concepts.

- Encourage students to engage in discussion both with the teacher and one another.

- Encourage student inquiry by asking thoughtful, open-ended questions and encourage students to ask questions of each other.

- Seek elaboration of students' initial responses.

- Engage students in experiences that might engender contradictions to their initial hypothesis and then encourage discussion.

- Allow wait time after posing questions.

- Provide time for students to construct relationships and create metaphors.

- Nurture children's natural curiosity through frequent use of the learning cycle model.

Source: Brookes and Brookes, 1993

In addition to the elements underpinning constructivism, co-constructivism involves a greater emphasis on collaborative learning. Learning tasks centre around dialogue (see Chapter 1) and include broader learning orientations, such as social and emotional dimensions. Co-constructivist learning is effective for:

- generating new knowledge;
- testing claims;
- learning social skills;
- building a community of learners.

The first three items on this list will be familiar to teachers; the fourth term is not so familiar. A community of learners is one of the main themes of the book that we referred to in Chapter 1 and now discuss in more depth.

A community of learners

Building a community of learners encourages all participants to be involved, invites complex learning and helps develop a language to talk about learning. Learning in this environment is complex because there are unanticipated outcomes, no right or wrong answers, the boundaries between learners and teachers are broken down; learning embraces personal-social as well as cognitive dimensions (see Table 2.3).

Table 2.3 *Features of a community of learners*

In a community of learners:

Students are:
- encouraged to engage in self-reflective learning;
- act as researchers who are responsible to some extent for defining their own knowledge and expertise.

Teachers:
- learn to provide instruction on a need to know basis.

The curriculum content:
- features a few recurring themes that students come to know at increasingly sophisticated levels of explanatory coherence and theoretical generality.

The environment:
- is designed to foster intentional learning not programmes, to encourage student reflection and discussion.

Modes of assessment:
- focus on the students' ability to discover and use knowledge.

Source: Brown and Campione, 1998: 158–61

In a community of learners the four themes used throughout the book – collaborative learning, responsibility, activity in learning and meta-learning – have particular significance.

Collaborative learning

Collaborative learning may take different forms, for example stronger and weaker examples. Co-construction encourages stronger forms of collaborative learning. These suggest equality of engagement (more or less equal contribution) and mutuality of engagement (extensive and connected discourse) (Damon and Phelps, 1989). These interactions require interdependence. Interdependence is about the ability to get to a point that could not be attained when learning alone. This is about complementing and building on others' views to generate shared knowledge (Crook, 1994). Some classrooms are set up to encourage independent or autonomous learners. In a community of learners there is encouragement of interdependence rather than autonomy or competition.

Weaker forms of collaboration do not rely on others and do not provide effective learning outcomes, for example working in a group in a collaborative activity (learning is assumed but may not be happening) but not engaged in collaborative learning (learning is made explicit).

Collaborative learning includes communicating effectively, providing mutual help, building trust and working on joint goals. In such a climate competition plays no major part. Competition can:

- discourage students who have few academic successes;
- discourage students from helping each other;
- encourage the cover up of misunderstandings;
- threaten peer relationships;
- segregate groups into higher- or lower-achieving students;
- encourage students to attribute success and failure to ability, rather than effort (Gipps, 1995).

Competition may encourage a performance orientation rather than a learning orientation (see Chapter 1). While competition may not lead to learning, conflict may. We take the view that difference and disagreement do not always lead to conflict. Indeed, living with ambiguity is an important aspect of complexity. However, learning may result in situations when there are disagreements in interpretation which can only be resolved through reflection (Crook, 1994). This may apply to group conflict. Conflict may also be internal which requires individual reflection.

In collaborative learning there are opportunities for learners to practise new roles and behaviours. These new behaviours make include risk-taking. Risk-taking is necessary as collaborative learning requires making intuitive and emerging ideas explicit (Crook, 1994). This is more likely to happen in an environment which is supportive and allows people to be unsure, tentative, doubt, question, challenge, make mistakes and change their minds.

The collaborative classroom will be less boundaried. Furniture arrangements will be flexible to allow young people and the teacher movement for different forms of activity and groupings. For example, there will be movement in and out of the classroom to the library and other locations for research.

Activity in learning

Activity in learning may also take different forms. In a learning community the form of activity needs to be based on young people acting as researchers, responsible for defining their own knowledge and expertise. Like collaboration, being involved in activity does not necessarily mean young people are learning. Young people need to reflect on the activity, identify what it is they are learning and then apply the understandings gained from the learning to inform future action; in other words, apply the learning cycle to the activity.

When asked about classroom learning young people say the most effective classroom activities are those that involve 'research, talking to other pupils, class discussions, demonstrations, practical work, group work and one to one help from the teacher' (Curtis, 2000: 6, based on Hughes, 1997). Where learners are involved in deciding the task, allowed to work in groups of their own choosing and free to move when appropriate, there is an observable

increase in motivation, co-operation and focus. This matches with the findings
of Mike Forret's case study.

A general impression emerges from other research that activities employed
most frequently by teachers are perceived by students to be less effective in
promoting their learning (Carnell, 2000; Cooper and McIntyre, 1996;
Hughes, 1997; Wallace, 1996). There is an inverse relationship between frequency of use and perceived effectiveness in developing learning: 'Classroom
activities are dominated by copying from the board or book and listening to
the teacher talk. What the students actually wanted was more balance, including group discussion and problem solving, a more brain-friendly environment, and the freedom to wander' (Crace, 2000: 48).

An important point, reinforced by these research studies, is the more central and dominant the teacher remains in the educational process, the more
dependent and docile the young people become (Bigge, 1982). Shifting the
balance to pupil interdependence and responsibility helps them become more
active and effective learners. There are important implications for the assessment of that learning and teachers need to consider congruent self-assessment activities. Using the *Do, Review, Learn and Apply* learning cycle may be
appropriate for part of the self and group assessment strategies.

Responsibility for learning

In a learning community responsibility for learning is shared. This is in contrast to most classroom practice. In classrooms designed on the reception
model of learning, young people usually do what is expected of them. There
is little choice and the teacher takes on more responsibility for what happens
than the learner. One way of shifting responsibility to young people in a community of learners, based on the co-construction model of learning, is for
teachers to provide instruction on a need-to-know basis (Brown and
Campione, 1998). For example, in Mike Forret's case study the young people
were responsible for:

- choosing the learning task;
- designing the task;
- managing their time;
- solving the problem;
- managing their conversations;
- managing the group dynamics;
- staying on task.

The teacher encouraged them in their endeavours, trusted them to learn collaboratively and use their time effectively. He helped them review their learning and make sense of their experiences.

Other research confirms that young people's learning is enhanced through
responsibility. Students prefer tasks where they are: 'engaged by the content
and by the approach which gave them a clear specification of task, consider-

ably more autonomy than they had been used to and challenged them to think' (Rudduck, 1991b: 36). Elsewhere it emerged that 'as young people acquire a view of themselves as active participants in their own learning, they then become more committed and effective as learners' (Carnell, 2000: 36). Claxton (1999) cites many other research projects in which learners are given greater responsibility for the initiation, direction, control and evaluation of their own learning. These sorts of learning experiences develop resilience, resourcefulness and reflection (see Chapter 1). As Claxton puts it:

> Just as a doctor or engineer learns their craft by gradually taking on more and more responsibility, so do learners in general. Finding ways to give young people experience of guiding their own learning is not a legacy from some liberal, child-centred ideology; it creates the practical conditions under which learning power develops. (Claxton, 1999: 294)

This has implications for classroom behaviour. Many teachers might express concern about giving pupils more responsibility for their learning. They may see this as lessening their control, and their fear is that the classroom may get out of control. In Chapter 8 in Peter Jarvis's case study one teacher expresses this concern. With the support of his colleagues he is able to give young people more responsibility for their learning. Initially there is some difficulty as the young people need to adjust to learning in a different way. This difficulty is short-lived. Where teachers give young people responsibility and trust them, as in Mike Forret's case, they choose challenging tasks and persevere. In Curtis's study there was a consensus that pupils 'behaved' when 'we're given something interesting to do', and 'teachers don't just shout at us' (Curtis, 2000: 9). Young people regard both the constraints of the classroom context on their behaviour (Carnell, 2000) and their own (mis)behaviour (Curtis, 2000) as blocks to learning (see also Watkins and Wagner, 2000).

Meta-learning (making sense of one's experiences of learning)

In a learning community young people are encouraged to engage in self-reflective learning (Brown and Campione, 1998). We suggest extending self-reflection to include meta-learning at both individual and group levels (see Chapter 1). In a learning community it is important to extend young people's understanding of collaborative learning at a meta-level. For example, the concepts of co-constructivism and interdependence need to be made explicit by using concrete examples in which social, emotional and cognitive aspects are addressed. We provide a set of prompts to encourage this strategy (see Table 2.4).

Language needs to foster a rich learning environment. The vocabulary and the formation of prompts focus on responsibility for learning, engagement, collaboration, trust, openness, risk-taking and change. It is a meta-learning language to help young people construct and develop meta-learning dialogue. Vocabulary is built which extends the capacity for learning. This is an example of what McNamee and Gergen (1999: xi) describe as 'meaningful

Table 2.4   *Some prompts for meta-learning*

Review
Identify significant ways group members learn together.

In what ways did the group members contribute to the task?

Learn
How has the group's conversation helped make connections and generate new ideas?

Analyse the ways in which the group is in control of its learning.

In what ways does risk-taking feature in the group?

What has been learned about the way the group is able to change and adapt, e.g. the extent to which the group is able to renegotiate learning goals?

Apply
What can group members do to enhance the conversation for learning and overcome blocks to learning?

Are there any ways in which the group could experiment to enable more effective learning, for example in managing conflict?

How can individual roles and responsibilities be shared for more effective group learning?

---

language generated within processes of relationship'. By offering prompts for dialogue there is a shared attempt to construct meaning and learning.

The highly structured approach suggested in the prompts in Table 2.4 may appear to limit creativity and spontaneity, but they provide a useful starting point. When young people become more experienced in learning conversations their dialogue is constructed by them and becomes gradually more complex and spontaneous.

As the prompts in Table 2.4 suggest this process is not a one-off. In further learning occasions young people may examine how the group deals with new tasks, learning goals or changed behaviours. This continuous cycle underscores the importance of the group taking responsibility for their decisions for change from an understanding of how their learning may be enhanced.

Collaborative learning, responsibility, activity in learning and meta-learning are not disconnected themes. They interrelate and occur concurrently in practice. In a community of learners it is important that young people reflect on these themes and understand their importance in learning. In other words they need to be addressed at a meta-level (see Figure 2.2).

Making the themes of collaborative learning, responsibility, activity in learning and meta-learning itself explicit helps learners deconstruct their experiences. In deconstructing them these themes are understood in relation to the purposes of learning, strategies for learning, effects of learning, feelings while learning, social relations and the context of learning (see Chapter 1). This meta-learning dialogue supports co-constructivism and the development of a learning community.

We have developed Brookes and Brookes's (1993) idea of providing constructivist strategies for teachers and suggest ten features in developing

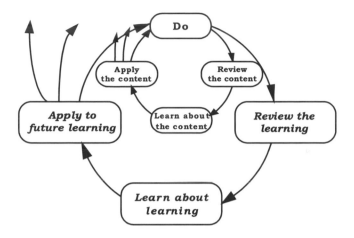

Figure 2.2   *A meta-learning cycle* (Watkins, 2001)

co-constructivist classrooms (see Table 2.5). The focus is not on the teacher's responsibility; learning is seen as a shared responsibility. But there are implications for the teacher to enable this to happen; the teacher's role here is to manage the learning, not be responsible for it.

Factors inhibiting a rich learning environment

Our experiences and Forret's and Claxton's research indicates that secondary school classrooms are more likely to encourage learners in the reception

Table 2.5   *Features in developing co-constructivist classrooms*

In co-constructivist classrooms

- the focus is on learning not on teaching; reciprocal teaching occurs – teachers are viewed as learners and pupils as teachers;
- all participants identify joint goals, plan activities and group tasks that require interdependence while allowing for individual responsibility;
- the pace is appropriate to the learning;
- language focuses on learning and meta-learning;
- learning is connected across all contexts; boundaries are permeated;
- learners construct their own questions, help each other develop their ideas through investigation, research, oral history and presentations;
- learning is seen as dialogue;
- learning is seen as holistic involving social, emotional as well as cognitive aspects;
- the idea of a learning community is fostered through goals, tasks, activities and social structures;
- there are many different sources to challenge the learners' thinking and take their learning forward.

---

model of learning. We do not take a critical or blaming stance but look to the wider social contexts to explain constraints on developing rich learning environments. The following case study reveals a teacher's struggle to maintain rich learning experience in the classroom.

Case study 2   'Stand and deliver'

What happens to teachers near examination time? We cram. We stand and deliver. We teach students to jump through hoops whose dimensions we have not set. Resultant pedagogies lead to crude *ventriloquy*: students learn to be operated by academic discourses rather than operating them.

As an illustration, here is the story of a recent Monday.

During Lesson One, I ask five 13-year-olds to write a hierarchical Person Specification for their ideal teacher. Unanimously voted Quality Number One is *someone who listens*. Number Two is *someone who explains clearly*. Number Three is *someone who allows us our own opinions*. It is a heartening start to the week. I make silent vows.

I then spend Lesson Two with a low ability class finishing coursework for their imminent GCSE examination in English. I ask them what they think of *Macbeth* and assume the listening position. They ask me to tell them what to think so that they can write it down and hand it back to me. The votive candles splutter.

Lesson Three is a meeting with the head teacher. I have just submitted targets for the department's end of Key Stage 3 external assessments. We appear to have committed ourselves to a 3 per cent increase on last year's results with an arguably weaker cohort. I leave his office and march down the corridor calculating how many lessons we have left with that year group before the examinations.

Lesson Four is with that very year group. I pinch their noses and ladle the content into them. Restlessly they copy yet another examination mantra from the board. One of them asks me 'When are we going to *do* something?' By and large, they indulge my panic. I have a growing sensation that I am selling them short.

Why was it is so difficult for me to adhere to the vows of Lesson One? That is how I want to teach: I know it is the best way. Yet what I want to do, or can do, or think is best becomes subordinate to doing what I'm told. The stories I tell myself about my teaching are edited out under pressure from the stories I'm told about *delivery*.

Source: Sullivan, 2000: 79–80

John Sullivan's case study demonstrates that under external pressure this teacher takes up a 'stand and deliver' position in the classroom adopting the transmission model of teaching; transmission equals delivery. Others concur: 'As the National Curriculum and Standard Assessment Tests engulf school work, right down to reception classes, they will supply new meaning and social purpose to school work. However, there is a danger that teachers may find themselves working with pupils in even more instrumental ways' (Wallace, 1996: 68). Shifting from the dominant transmission model of teaching to a richer learning environment may feel like working against the grain.

As John Sullivan's case study shows, young people may expect or accept the reception view of themselves as learners and expect the teachers to deliver. The pupil understands what is expected and conforms to the appropriate role. This is borne out elsewhere:

> I sometimes sit down and work on my own, I sometimes work with others, I sometimes ask the teacher for help. It depends. I am not worried about getting a higher grade. I am more interested in getting a good reputation.
> Q: A good reputation?
> Just to sit down and get on with your work quietly and not run around the classroom. (Boy, Year 8, from Carnell, 2000: 58)

Getting a good reputation, in this young person's view, is about 'performing' as a model student. Expectations here of learning in a secondary school classroom are of pupils working quietly, alone, sitting at their desks and waiting for the teacher to direct activities. Note also how this boy describes what he does as *work* rather than *learning* and the work is done quietly to please the teacher. This is an example of a 'strategic learner' (Ertmer and Newby, 1996) – someone who uses their knowledge about themselves and about the task or context to deliberately select strategies to achieve the desired goal. In this case the learner selects a superficial approach to learning to match context expectations (Carnell, 2000). In other situations being strategic would be embracing complexity and trying a range of different strategies as demonstrated in Mike Forret's case study.

Claxton and John Sullivan warn of the constant pressure to move on and to document progress that results in bite-sized tasks. This denies young people:

- opportunities to experience making slow progress on complicated, ill-formulated tasks and to find out what that feels like;
- pleasure in cumulative progress;
- opportunities to develop resilience, that is, 'strengthening the learning muscles that sustained engagement requires' (Claxton, 1999: 282–3).

The boys in Forret's case study were able to identify the constraints of other experiences in school. They pointed to lack of challenge, time restrictions and the resultant short chunks of easy to solve classroom activity. There are enormous implications for curriculum design both at classroom level and whole school level in supporting rich learning environments both for teachers and young people.

A set of inhibiting forces and contradictions, internal and external, prevent teachers from working with young people in ways they would like, as can be seen in John Sullivan's case study. In addition, in attempting to maintain control, teachers might curtail the potential for participation in discussion and participatory activities, and make the work easy, unemotional and non-controversial (McNeil, 1986).

The organization of school life has remained relatively unchanged for the last hundred years compared with, for example, the organization of work.

With the advance of technology the office can be open 24 hours, seven days a week and may not be located in a single site. Schools are slow to embrace the changes new technology offers, so we like the appropriate title of Cuban's (1993) article 'Computers meet classroom: classroom wins'. There is huge potential for school to help young people learn in completely different ways but there needs to be a change in conception about classroom learning and the roles of the teacher and learner. If conceptions do not change then learning will not change.

Closing thoughts

The research presented in this chapter indicates that young people have important insights in understanding the classroom as a context for learning, so we conclude by suggesting that teachers consult with young people about their learning experiences. Engaging young people in dialogue about their classroom experience is one way of developing a learning community. This not only helps learners become more effective but also provides teachers with important information about the most effective ways of supporting young people's learning.

Classrooms are complex places. In promoting a rich learning environment for the twenty-first century classrooms may become even more complex as they encourage the following:

- a shift in responsibility from teachers to young people;
- a focus on learning and a learning language;
- a shift in the teachers' role from a behaviour manager to a learning manager;
- a shift in the young person's role as a researcher and learning partner with other learners;
- an emphasis on reciprocal teaching and learning;
- a view that the territory of the classroom is a shared learning space;
- more permeable classroom boundaries.

These strategies encourage richer conceptions of learning and the development of a learning community to support effective learning. In the next chapter we consider how school can block the learning for some children.

Further reading

Claxton, G. (1999) *Wise Up*. London: Bloomsbury.
Hughes, M. (1997) *Lessons Are for Learning*. Stafford: Network Educational Press.
Watkins, C. (2001) *Learning about Learning Enhances Performance*. National School Improvement Network Research Matters No 13. London: University of London, Institute of Education.
Watkins, C., Carnell, E., Lodge, C., Wagner, P. and Whalley, C. (2000) *Learning about Learning: Resources for Supporting Effective Learning*. London: Routledge Falmer.

3
Learning at Risk

In every school there are young people whose learning is at risk. By 'at risk' we mean that they may experience overwhelming distractions, interference or blocks to their learning. This may be temporary, for example because they witnessed an accident on the way to school. It may be more long lasting as a result of a more serious event such as the death of a loved one. The risk may arise from ongoing experiences, such as bearing the burdens of being a young carer, and may include those for whom the school has exhausted their possible responses. This chapter is concerned with the school's response to young people's learning being at risk. There is a tension for staff members of the school. They may feel that they wish to include all young people, but the difficulties and behaviour of some young people can make that hard. There may not be enough time to respond to the needs of the individual. Structures and systems may be inappropriate for the young people and may further alienate and make difficulties for them. Hamblin, writing in 1978, suggested that schools are set up for the good kids. We argue that with the current pressure on schools to improve the overall school performance this is even more the case.

Barber (1996) considers that one of the most urgent problems for secondary schooling is the large proportion of young people who are the disappeared, the disaffected or the disappointed. He quotes evidence from the Keele University survey that suggests the disappeared may be as many as 8–15 per cent of young people, and as they do not attend school or any other establishments they have disappeared from the official view and attention. Over 10,000 children are excluded temporarily or permanently from school every year. A further 10–15 per cent, Barber claims, are disaffected and may frequently bunk off school from time to time, making it harder for them to gain continuity in their learning experiences. Up to 60 per cent of pupils frequently count the minutes to the end of the lesson – these are the disappointed. Barber argues that young people need 'intellectually challenging and varied curriculum taught by enthusiastic and talented teachers' (Barber, 1996: 88) who pay more attention to the young people themselves.

This chapter is constructed around contributions from expert practitioners in different fields. First, we consider how one school helped a refugee, Danijel, who was at risk in the school. Second, we present the approach of an educational psychologist who considers how she can best support teachers working with young people at risk. Third, we have included the reflections of a headteacher who works with young people from profoundly damaging situations. Finally, we look at parental responses to schools' efforts with their children. Each of these contributions considers the implications for schools in putting the learning of the young people first.

The themes of this chapter

The first theme that runs through this chapter, and the whole book, is the need to take account of the context for young people's learning. This refers to the physical context, both inside and out of school. But it also refers to their emotional and domestic context. We want to stress that young people interact with their environment, including with the school. If we only consider the young person when they are causing us concern then we will miss aspects of their difficulties, and aspects over which we may have some control and some power to change. In order to consider this wide perspective, we need to involve a range of people: teachers, others working in school such as classroom assistants or playground supervisors, parents, classmates and friends, professionals from outside and, not least, the young person themselves.

The second theme arises from the first. We need dialogue between those involved in order to empower those who can change the context for the young person at risk. This dialogue will bring together different perspectives, perceptions, knowledge, and produce suggestions, plans, solutions and ways forward that would not be thought of by one person alone. One could liken this dialogue to a small learning community focused on helping the young person at risk return to learning.

The third theme is that as all learning is messy and complex. Supporting young people whose learning is seriously at risk is likely to be highly complex and even more messy. Complexity arises from the range of interacting factors which may need to be considered (see the example of the refugee, Danijel). The young person is likely to be changing in response to their discomfort and difficulties. This suggests that the blocks they are experiencing may also be complex, and consequently the solutions and ways forward are hard to identify and may not always appear to be working.

These themes all relate to looking for patterns of behaviour and reactions, for the need to monitor and review the situation with a young person at risk. Responses and plans will need to be flexible. Underlying all these themes is a concern to ensure that some of the most difficult blocks to learning are alleviated by the school wherever possible. The school will need to keep an eye on how they are responding to such young people, to see whether they can alter their procedures and structures or attend to their relationships in order to lessen the risk for young people. Some of the behaviour management strategies we have seen assume that all young people are capable of exercising choices, which is not the case. There is also a belief that young people learn from punishment and from examples made of others. This is also not the case.

We begin with the story of a refugee, Danijel. Many people working in and with urban schools will recognize elements of his story, and have experienced the difficulties described here in trying to help youngsters like him become learners in their school. Danijel's story has a happy outcome thanks to the combined efforts of members of the school community. Alison Heap works with schools to ensure that they support young refugees in schools in her local education authority (LEA).

Example   Danijel
Alison Heap, ethnic minority achievement adviser

Danijel joined Year 7 in November. At his admission interview, a Croatian interpreter helped the head of year to establish that his family had recently arrived from Denmark where they had spent a year in a refugee camp. Danijel's parents, aunt and English-speaking cousin were in London with him. Danijel had not been to school in Croatia, had attended the school in the camp in Denmark intermittently and had suffered from serious illness as a child from which he had recovered well. Danijel spoke no English at all.

The head of year informed staff and the tutor group of Danijel's imminent admission and ensured that Danijel's entitlements (free school meals, uniform grant and bus pass) would be in place. She also arranged for a small group of students from the tutor group to be trained as 'class friends' in preparation for Danijel's admission. Their initial role, working as a team on a rota basis, would be to ensure that Danijel did not get lost, that he would be helped to find his way around the school and would be introduced to each teacher. Subsequently the students would continue to keep an eye out for the new boy and to check on his progress. The class friends were asked to debrief the tutor at the end of each day for the first couple of weeks, on how things were going for Danijel and to discuss any concerns.

During the first few weeks all went well. Responses to a round robin progress report circulated to all subject staff suggested that Danijel had settled in well. At an admission review meeting (attended by the same interpreter) the family were given positive feedback on Danijel's settling in period.

However, a few weeks later several concerns about Danijel came to light. First, his tutor had heard from the school meals supervisor that Danijel was less than enthusiastic about his lunch, rarely eating more than a few mouthfuls. Second, Danijel had shown little progress in acquiring spoken English and the ethnic minority achievement language support teacher who worked with Danijel in a number of curriculum areas suspected that Danijel had a hearing problem.

Danijel had missed out on the routine health screening for his tutor group during their first half term, so arrangements were made for him to have a hearing test. The results show that he did indeed have a significant hearing loss and would need to be fitted with hearing aids. However, the acquisition of his first language appeared to have been unaffected so it was thought likely that his English language acquisition would continue normally when the hearing aids were issued. Subject teachers were also reminded by the special educational needs co-ordinator (SENCO) about the measures they should take to ensure full access and involvement of students with hearing loss and were given information about Danijel's specific hearing impairment.

In addition, the tests by the school nurse revealed that Danijel had serious dental problems that were preventing him eating certain foods. Danijel's parents were invited to come in to discuss his dental treatments and diet. They were given advice and appointments for treatment. Danijel's cousin acted as interpreter at this discussion.

In the mean time Danijel was showing real talent in design and technology (D&T) lessons and his teacher, the head of D&T, made a point of praising his work and took the opportunity to exhibit one of Danijel's pieces of work in a year assembly and at a parents' evening. In addition a routine discussion of the tutor group by all its subject teachers allowed this teacher to speak of Danijel's ability and to encourage other subject teachers to build on his abilities in problem solving and practical activities. Danijel was also encouraged to attend the D&T weekly homework club so that he could take advantage of specialist support in his written work.

At this stage Danijel, who had generally been regarded as a popular new admission to the tutor group, suddenly started to be involved in playground incidents. On several occasions he was named as a participant in fights at break time and had been involved when a window had been broken after school. The tutor's investigations and conversations with the students who had earlier acted as class friends revealed that Danijel had become involved with a student whose behaviour had long been causing concern. This student's name appeared in reports of all these incidents. Further investigations established that Danijel was being bullied by this student and 'dared' to take part in incidents. Sanctions were imposed and Danijel's behaviour was closely monitored. Two of the class friends volunteered to spend time with Danijel on a regular basis. This soon resulted in Danijel becoming a library monitor and a long-standing friendship developed between Danijel and one of the class friends.

A week later a letter about a geography trip was sent to the parents and guardians of all Year 7 students. Unusually Danijel's parents did not send in the required permission for him to participate. The tutor therefore arranged a meeting with the family at short notice to investigate this breakdown in communication and to discuss the various recent developments that had taken place. The school was relying on Danijel's older cousin to attend the meeting and act as interpreter. When the family did not attend the tutor arranged to visit Danijel's home with the interpreter who had attended the admissions meeting.

During this home visit it emerged that Danijel's cousin had been refused asylum and he and his mother had been repatriated. Danijel's parents felt that Danijel had been badly affected by this and it might explain why his behaviour had deteriorated. As a result of the repatriation the family were to be rehoused and the school was able to recommend to the housing department that the family should be allocated a smaller local property so that Danijel would not have to start all over again in a new school.

The previous communication with Danijel's family was re-established and his behaviour improved. He also talked to his language support teacher about the departure of his cousin and aunt and his anxiety about his parents' asylum application, still under Home Office consideration. He brought in letters and photographs sent by his cousin to show his teacher and closest friend.

The school now has made plans to introduce Circle Time (see Chapter 9) in Year 8 in an attempt to build up collective responsibility amongst students within each tutor group. Because new bilingual and asylum-seeking students are being admitted to the school increasingly often, there are also plans to produce a welcome booklet in community languages giving new students and their parents and carers information about the school. In addition Year 7 students are to produce a *Welcome* photograph album with captions in community languages so that new students can become more familiar with the school environment prior to admission. The students will take photographs of all aspects of school life as part of a PSHE project.

A contribution made by Danijel in a small group during the last PSHE lesson of the summer term gave clear evidence of his progress and confidence and paid tribute to the work the school had done to support him. Danijel said, 'I think Year 8 will be good. I like my friends and my teachers. Everyone helps me'.

Ethnic Minority Achievement Central Team (LCAS Development), London Borough of Enfield

---

We include this example because it is a story of successful support for a student who could so easily have found himself in a situation that made it impossible for him to continue as a learner in the school. It illustrates the implications of all three of our themes: the young person's context was kept in mind, and various people brought together in dialogues about helping him, and the solutions took account of the complexity of the situation and allowed the school to learn and change their practice. For a while he was moving rapidly towards a situation that could have put him outside the school. Alison Heap comments that it is important that all students have opportunities to develop relationships outside the classroom, for example with class friends. Similarly staff need to take every opportunity to praise students and to demonstrate their strengths to other teachers, as the D&T teacher did for Danijel. She reflects on the contribution of the school to the happy outcome of Danijel's difficulties. While Danijel is unusual in having had several interrelated health problems that affected his learning, his case demonstrates the importance of:

- ensuring that students' needs are closely monitored;
- routine and continual health screening;
- rapid follow up of concerns;
- establishing and maintaining good communications between refugee and asylum-seeking families, the school and outside agencies (particularly the use of translation and interpreting with bilingual families);
- teaching and non-teaching staff in close and regular communication about behaviour and learning;
- the role of class friends in supporting individuals and monitoring their needs;

- using Circle Time and PSHE programmes to support the development of the learning community;
- learning from the experience to improve the school's induction procedures for student admissions.

It is significant that the school did not lose sight of the need to help Danijel become a learner in their school and were able to attend to some of the difficulties of his situation. The hard work that the staff and classmates undertook at these early stages of Danijel's career in school to support and establish him in the community will pay dividends. Such work is crucial when students are admitted late in their school career.

Danijel's example also illustrates another significant point. Young people do not occupy static or fixed positions as learners. Even the most enthusiastic and effective learner can experience learning difficulties. Teachers and systems need to be flexible and allow for these changing situations.

We have chosen to include our second example, from an educational psychologist, because in it Patsy Wagner emphasizes the value of consultation with the teachers of the school. She rejects the idea that educational psychologists can wave a 'magic wand' to change the young person at risk. Patsy Wagner is an educational psychologist in the London Borough of Kensington and Chelsea, and the following extract is taken from a talk she gave to teachers.[1]

Example   Educational psychologists in consultation with schools
Patsy Wagner, educational psychologist

The model I've been using of the way an educational psychologist (EP) can work with a school is called *consultation*. An educational psychologist needs to be a teacher and it is helpful to remember that this person is an educational psychologist not a psychiatrist, because many people still get the two muddled up. We are teachers who have done additional training in children's learning and development. We work with teachers to try and help teachers help children progress in school. That's our core function in relation to schools.

When I started to train in 1978 a book had just been written called *Reconstructing Educational Psychology* (Gillham, 1978). It talked about all the things that EPs might do. David Hargreaves wrote a chapter in it and talked about an interactionist perspective on deviance and how you couldn't use 'within-the-person' models – you had to think about situations because behaviour varies across situations. You need to try and find patterns within situations in order to try and change behaviour.

The Code of Practice is providing opportunities for more creative ways of working, which is certainly something that more services are looking for. Those of you who do know some educational psychologists may well know some very interesting, creative practitioners, but the whole service doesn't yet work that way. I'd like to look now at a way of working in school.

The model I am going to look at is called consultation. I am going to look at some of the assumptions about working this way which is working together in a more collaborative fashion rather than working separately, which is very often how EPs work.

- Pupils have a right to education as part of their peer group, not segregated from it.
- The effects of segregation diminish us. Probably more so with young people. Children in school who have the advantage of mixing with a range of children are advantaged in a way that we are not.
- Schools make a difference and different schools make different differences, in quite subtle ways. So particular groups within a school might do better or worse in different areas. If there are those differences among pupils then some of the reasons for those differences must be there within school and it must be possible to work on them.
- Teachers are skilled professionals and by taking children away we are implying that they are not. They are implying that we (EPs) have a magic wand and certainly EPs know that we don't, and we feel distressed that after we have been in to see a child they say 'he's still the same, obviously it didn't work' the next time they see us.
- Teachers' goals are linked to success. We are there to help kids to succeed. Teaching is complex and demanding, it's not an easy job. It's one of the most complex jobs that any of us know and doing it well is not easy. Doing it well means addressing the complexities and the challenges systematically. Helping some pupils succeed in school is more challenging than helping others. We are not going to 'fix' some of them. They are not going to change dramatically, but we may find ways of helping kids through the education system in a way that means that they do go through it. They don't have to be excluded from mainstream education.
- EPs are not direct agents of change for individual pupils. In other words, an EP seeing a child is rarely going to make a difference to that individual. They're in school maybe once a month. It is going to be much more likely that the head of year or form tutor or class teacher who knows the child well is going to make a difference, because that person has the contact.

Consultation is what I am going to talk about, consultation as a meeting of peers with different sets of skills. The rationale for working in this way is that the teacher is the person who is most concerned. She or he has the professional responsibility to be concerned, unlike the child whose behaviour may be influenced by discomfort. They are the people in daily contact with the young person and they are working in the context in which the problem arises. It was way back in the Warnock Report that we were reminded that special needs are relative to context. They are not absolute. The context is important and makes a difference. These things are not within the person. That's one of the major dilemmas over the assessment procedures that look within the person. It is also the context that can be adapted and changed. That is why different schools make different differences. The teacher is the person with professional responsibility for young people and so is best placed to be the agent of change. I am not saying that this will happen without resources, but there is a process that needs to be gone through to get things to work for the young person.

The EP on the other hand is the person who visits the school and, because of that, has some perspective on the context of the school. Very often when you are very involved in something you cannot see the broader perspective. So there are two advantages to the idea of the EP being the person who works with the teacher. They are someone who has a perspective because they are not located in the school. But they are on the boundaries. They should know enough about the school to be able to make some sense of the system and how it works. They should also be able to help because they have some training in making sense of individuals, groups and organizational issues, and the links between those sorts of things. They have some skills in problem exploration and processes of problem exploration with teachers.

I think this is the key – the process of problem exploration. I think that the actual process of helping teachers do some problem-solving is the most creative thing one can do. It could be with the year team, or department team or planning team. The focus could be individuals or it could be a group or class or organizational issue. For example, I've been working in a primary school where there is a very big boy who just goes around knocking every one down. The consultation originally started over him. It led to the idea that there might be a need for a consultation about a group because it led to the question 'Is it just him?' and no, it wasn't. It was a whole group of boys, but he was clumsy and he stood out. This led to the question 'Where does it happen?' and in fact it happened in the playground. That particular line of consultation led to training all the playground supervisors in that school. An individual is always part of a group and this kind of investigation can sometimes lead to patterns shifting much more quickly. It is about school- and classroom-focused investigation and problem-solving.

Because schools are social systems the psychology needs to be a social psychology and not a within-the-person model. So therefore psychodynamic theory does not fit very well. And behaviourism is an individual model. The psychology that does make sense is Kelly's construct theory – how people make sense of the world and manage themselves in the world. Symbolic interactionism is also useful – looking at the determinants of behaviour rather than saying that someone is that sort of person. We might see a child behave in one way with a particular peer group and another with a different group. So we are looking for patterns in behaviour. The third strand is systems thinking, both about families and about how you can translate ideas about systems in families to schools.

London Borough of Kensington and Chelsea

In this talk Patsy Wagner emphasizes the importance of not seeing the problems and difficulties as located within the young person. She reminds us that schools can make different differences and therefore the school must look at the young person in their context. The idea of consultation, of pooling complementary skills, is very significant here and relates to the second theme of dialogue. The teachers have a professional concern and the daily contact with the young person. The EP brings important knowledge about the school and some ways of thinking which are to do with linking the young person and their context. This complementarity of roles enables the dialogue, the consultation, for planning support for the young person and helps all concerned to deal with complexity.

We now present a third set of examples which consider how easy it is for members of the school community to block learning for young people experiencing emotional, behavioural and social difficulties (EBSD). The young people described here do not have such happy outcomes in their stories, and Sally Wells has met them since they left mainstream school.

Example   Children with emotional, behavioural and social difficulties at risk in mainstream schools
Sally Wells, Principal of Child and Youth Care Education Service

Current educational direction in England and Wales would appear to put more importance on academic achievement rather than on social and emotional literacy. Young people who experience emotional, behavioural and social difficulties are often unable to learn in the same way as their peers. Children who are deeply traumatized or emotionally distressed cannot invest in learning. There is some recent evidence to suggest that children who have experienced emotional, physical and/or sexual abuse actually suffer brain damage. How then can these young people manage successfully in an atmosphere where academic attainment and expectations of conformity are paramount?

Children who have had their sense of self-worth removed by adults through abusive or neglectful practices find many school practices hard to attend to when they have other, more pressing and painful things on their minds. They must attend school every day, remember to wear school uniform, obey school rules, bottle up their anger and fear, deal with peer group pressure, pay attention in lessons, complete homework and communicate appropriately with a large number of adults and children. The decreasing possibility for pastoral staff to make regular twice-daily welfare checks on pupils means that problems build up without vulnerable pupils receiving robust but compassionate guidance when they need it. In some schools this can lead to a pattern of sanctions, non-attendance, temporary exclusion and, finally, permanent exclusion. Support in most schools is aimed at children who know how to behave but need the assistance of certain sets of boundaries to help them keep on the right path. Those pupils who break the rules or who are unable to conform to them are often punished, without adults understanding the emotional and intellectual chaos in which those pupils are living.

Last year a Year 7 boy was stopped on the stairs in his comprehensive school, in front of a number of other pupils. This boy was being consistently physically abused by his father at home, and had just been taken into care and was residing in a local children's home. The teacher said, 'You are wearing a round earring instead of a stud. Take it out.' 'No.' 'Do as I say. You are just a little boy in a big school and I am the teacher.' This remark caused the boy – already with few feelings of self-worth – to reply 'F—off.' The boy was temporarily excluded. Upon his return to school he experienced a number of similar incidents and was soon permanently excluded. He was without schooling for several months. His assessment for a statement of special educational needs was halted because he was not in a school. At present he is still not in school, several months later, and is causing immense problems in his children's home.

The way the National Curriculum is interpreted in many schools does not allow for the young person who has little self-esteem, who has a fear of competition, who has missed a lot of school through non-attendance or being moved around because of being in care. The belief by teachers that they must cover content means that they focus more on content than on the individual young person. There are plenty of young people, both in and out of care, who have been to seven or eight primary schools and three or four secondary schools. These young people know they will perform poorly in standard assessment tasks (SATs) and other tests and examinations, not because they are intellectually weak but because they cannot concentrate on tasks that seem temporarily irrelevant to them in the wider scheme of things. This expectation of poor performance leads to further feelings of lack of self-worth.

There is a misguided expectation in some schools that pupils can consume and reproduce information when experiencing emotional distress. All this compounds the problem of 'Learning to fail, failing to learn'. For many pupils experiencing EBSD there has been a failure by adults to diagnose and prescribe for conditions of educational and emotional difficulty. Combined with a lack of intelligent use of effective assessment materials and lack of sensitive child-centred resources within large schools, the emotionally and socially vulnerable pupil is at enormous risk of failure, further abuse and repeated rejection.

A Year 4 boy who suffered gross sexual abuse began to behave sexually inappropriately at school. The headteacher asked for a support worker to ensure that neither the boy, nor his peers, nor the staff were at risk during the school day. This was not deemed possible, as the boy had no statement. The headteacher eventually had to exclude the boy. The statementing process has not begun, as the boy is not in a school. He cannot be considered for a therapeutic placement as he is not statemented.

There is now little time or space for nurturing environments within the comprehensive school.

A Year 9 boy came to our service after being without schooling for four months. He had been taken into care after suffering gross physical and sexual abuse. He was difficult to engage, being surly and defiant and physically challenging, but he was very interested in most school subjects. He wanted to control his own timetable and much of the work done with him was to try and get him to do things the teacher asked of him so that he could return to mainstream schooling. On one occasion he pushed the teacher violently in the chest and face and his education support worker (ESW) was brought in to talk to the boy. He refused to look at or talk to the ESW, addressing remarks to him through the headteacher. The ESW realized there was something wrong and asked why the boy was angry with him. The boy was upset that the ESW had not visited on Open Day four weeks previously. The ESW accompanied the boy to his classroom, sat down with him and looked at all his work. During this time the boy put his foot gently against that of the ESW. The ESW put his arm out on the table and the boy put his arm gently against it. The boy calmed down, apologized to all concerned and was able to continue successfully with his work the rest of that week.

In mainstream schools there is pressure on staff and pupils to perform well, to raise academic standards, to do better than before, to beat the national average. There are many young people who have been poorly treated by adults who have no investment in learning for the time being. Schools are set up to help children learn academically rather than emotionally, to improve literacy and numeracy rather than communication skills and problem-solving, to make children control themselves rather than admit to and deal with the feelings of hurt and anger and fear inflicted on them by adults.

> *A Year 8 girl who had experienced physical abuse and emotional neglect from her mother since she was a toddler began to act sexually inappropriately as she approached puberty. There were also incidents of self-harm, and as a result she had treatment from the local Child and Mental Health Service team. She was referred to a psychiatric unit, and in the mean time moved into a children's home with education on site. Her authority then proposed she should move back into mainstream education, although the small school unit she attended recommended that she be assessed for a statement of special educational needs. This was refused, and despite the fact that she has made allegations against male workers, the girl is now being transported by a male taxi-driver to and from her mainstream school that is an hour away. This young person has missed a year of mainstream education, experiences enormous emotional and behavioural difficulties, and has been returned without preparation to a large comprehensive school where she receives no more support than other pupils. The risk factor to the girl is enormous.*
>
> When EBSD children cannot operate within the system they are often sent away, temporarily or permanently. They may find themselves in a special school with other children who are angry and confused, or sent away to a residential school. They may find themselves in Education Otherwise or without any schooling at all. Many young people who experience EBSD desperately need a place of safety where they can feel understood, cared for, cared about, guided and, above all, secure. Mainstream schools are not, in general, places of sanctuary for the abused, the neglected, the fearful and the angry child.
>
> Child and Youth Care Education Service, attached to Boys and Girls Welfare Society, Cheadle, Cheshire

These examples from Sally Wells illustrate young people experiencing emotional, behavioural and social difficulties, whose learning is at risk in mainstream schools. Young people are profoundly affected by their context and in turn have an impact upon the school. The complexity of their situation is evident to all those who come into contact with them. However, in many cases the school structures and systems are not taking enough account of the complexity in the lives of these young people, and not adapting their systems to accommodate the needs of these young people. However, there are, as we have said, some young people for whom learning at school is an impossibility for some of the time.

We refer in Chapter 1 to the tensions for school communities in trying to provide for all young people (the inclusion policy) whilst also responding to external pressures for higher test performances. This tension may work against the interest of young people whose learning is at risk. The risks result from:

- the National Curriculum being tied to the age of the student, so it may not be developmentally appropriate or relevant to the child's situation;
- an emphasis on performance because of the pressure for the school to perform well in league tables;
- more importance being attached to coverage of subject knowledge than to emotional and social development;
- the bureaucracy of the statementing process that does not always serve the needs of young people, their families or their schools.

As Patsy Wagner observed, schools make different differences. This means schools must consider what they are contributing to the situation, and how this can be improved for the young person. Schools could consider what they could do to avoid contributing to the risk for young people. This might include:

- pastoral staff monitoring patterns of behaviour and progress in young people and reviewing these frequently (as in Danijel's story);
- pastoral staff ensuring that 'robust but compassionate guidance' is given when the students need it;
- behaviour policies being flexible and taking account of students who may have difficulties and who are not being deliberately disruptive if they do not conform;
- understanding students' limited ability to learn when experiencing emotional distress;
- some young people at risk have their lives run by many different adults; it is important that communication between them is clear, consistent, proactive and pragmatic;
- diagnosing and prescribing for conditions of educational and emotional development;
- taking account of the emotional toll of responding to difficult behaviour in an objective manner which does not exacerbate the situation;
- recognizing that time and sensitivity often solve emotional problems, enabling young people to trust adults and be able to receive learning from them.

These observations connect to one theme of this chapter, that schools need to consider how their structures and procedures are relating to and impacting on young people at risk. Teachers hold different beliefs about how flexible schools should be and many express a belief that they should treat all young people the same. However, where needs are different, these must be differently met.

Closing thoughts

We end this chapter with some thoughts about consultation with parents and taking account of the views of young people themselves. Schools need to work with the parents of young people at risk. Some schools manage this much better than others. One parent contrasts a negative experience where her daughter was asked to leave her secondary school, with her subsequent experience in the next school where a very satisfactory outcome for her daughter was achieved.

> She was quite a troublesome child. They couldn't wait to get rid of her. She went to (. . . School) after that, and she was still difficult but they were just so understanding and caring and really tried to help us. It was 'Let's have a look at the situation. Let's see what we can do', and in the meetings, 'Why do you think you're doing

these things?' There was more discussion and negotiation. It was human and not patronizing either to the child or me. Whereas at the other school they were extremely patronizing. (Parent of 17-year-old girl, quoted in Askew, 2000: 112)

Another parent comments that useful strategies involve dialogue between parents and teachers.

The best ones [schools] are the ones that say: 'I am working on a strategy to get your child to do this and it would be good if you could do this.' Actually tell you the educational aims and give you the sort of information you might need to try and support what is going on. Ask you what you suggest. (Parent of 14-year-old boy, quoted in Askew, 2000: 112)

We are not arguing that teachers must take individual responsibility for helping young people at risk, but we wish to draw attention to the implications of the examples in this chapter. The teacher will best help young people at risk when they are aware that:

- there are differences between the young people they meet;
- they need to see a child holistically, in the context of their home, social group, emotional development and so forth;
- young people do not occupy static or fixed positions;
- the situation is likely to be complex and messy, and so are the ways of moving forward;
- the child can be anywhere on a continuum from enthusiastically engaged to disaffected and difficult.

In Chapter 9 we quote a list of what a group of Year 8 students wanted from their 'Good Teacher'. We note that among the points they included are some that indicate that they want teachers who put human beings first. They want someone who will listen, is forgiving, perseveres with them, encourages them, has faith in them, makes allowances and 'helps you when you're stuck' (MacBeath, 1999: 60).

School provides a significant part of learning for most children but in this chapter we recognize that for some young people schools are places where they cannot learn, temporarily or otherwise. Schools need to ensure that their actions, policies, procedures and structures do not add to the risk of these young people being excluded from school, and that everything possible is done to ensure that the young person's entitlement to learn in school is honoured. We realize that some young people are in such complex and difficult situations that they are unable to learn in school, and may endanger the learning of others. This may be because these young people are responding to 'discomfort', to use Patsy Wagner's word.

We have devoted a chapter to considering connecting young people's learning across the boundaries of the school (see Chapter 6). We have emphasized the role of the pastoral team in helping young people learn. If young people are not learning then it is important that this is identified and support given within school, and external agencies notified if necessary (see Chapter 7). To support young people, when the learning is at risk, the school will be using its structures, processes and relationships to identify and solve the problems (see Chapter 9 and Watkins and Wagner, 2000).

In this chapter we have considered in general terms the situation for young people whose learning may be blocked. We have referred to the necessity of taking into account how the context is influencing the young person. This context includes the interaction with the school's structures, processes and relationships. It may also include health and personal issues. The complexity of the context for some young people means that the support provided by the school needs to take account of this complexity, and will be best developed through dialogue among those who can bring a range of perspectives, skills and knowledge to the situation. For schools, teachers and the young people themselves developing strategies to minimize the risks can be challenging and take time and patience.

Note

1 A version of this talk appeared in Askew and Carnell (1996).

Further reading

MacBeath, J. (1999) *Schools Must Speak for Themselves: The Case for School Self-Evaluation*. London: Routledge Falmer.
Watkins, C. and Wagner, P. (2000) *Improving School Behaviour*. London: Paul Chapman.

4
Tutors, Tutor Groups and Learning[1]

'Someone who tells them off and gives them stuff.' This was how one tutor described her role at a school staff development day. This chapter considers a more significant role that tutors can play in supporting the learning of their tutor groups. We consider the special position of the tutor in the school and how this can be used with their tutor group to support learning. The tutor could then better describe himself or herself as 'someone who helps them learn'.

Marland and Rogers captured some of the important aspects of the tutor's role as champion of the tutee when they wrote:

> The tutor is the heart of the school, the specialist whose specialism is bringing everything together, whose subject is the pupil herself, who struggles for the tutee's entitlement, and who enables the pupil to make best use of the school and develop her person. The tutor will be successful to the extent that he keeps this central vision in mind and builds out of it an over-arching pattern to which all the details relate. (Marland and Rogers, 1997: 12)

In this chapter we expand Marland and Roger's idea to suggest that the tutor's subject is the tutee *and* their learning. They indicate that the tutor plays an important part in this by helping the young person make best use of the school. We expand this to suggest that they can also help them become more effective learners by drawing on the tutor's special position in relation to the tutees and the school.

The experiences of many schools, supported by research, suggest that two factors are especially associated with supporting students' learning: the relationship between the tutor and the learner, and the focus on the students' learning. Some of the most improving schools in recent years have been developing these aspects of the tutor's role. But in other schools, in our experience, there is often little consideration or development of the role of the tutor in supporting young people's learning. One survey which covered 55 secondary schools, found that the role of tutor was not defined in most schools, but largely left to the individual tutor to establish (Megahy, 1998). This survey also found evidence that very few tutors (fewer than 15 per cent) see their work as relating directly to learning. Most see their role as reactive (about 30 per cent) or to do with care and welfare (more than 20 per cent).

In many secondary schools the tutor group is the basic group for learning at Key Stage 3 and for some core subjects in Key Stage 4. In many schools where these arrangements exist, the tutor remains with the tutor group as long as they are in the school. Other schools have a deliberate policy of mixing students from different classes in the tutor group. This second model has some benefits but in our view these do not outweigh the advantages of tutoring a group that has shared learning experiences over a period of time. However, the suggestions we make in this chapter do not depend on tutor groups being teaching groups. We consider how the tutor can use their group to focus on their learning and avoid too much admonition and administration.

Tutoring, of course, is not the sole preserve of the tutor. Many other staff in the school (not all teachers) may engage in activities that could be described as tutoring. We look explicitly at the role of the form or pastoral tutor while Chapter 5 focuses on individual learning conversations. In this chapter we are concerned with how the tutor can support the learning of the tutor group by considering the following:

- the tutor's special position;
- supporting the learning of the tutor group;
- communicating with other teachers;
- communicating with families;
- school issues in realizing effective tutoring for learning.

The tutor's special position

'Goals are often buried in the mundane,' commented a teacher on a course about tutoring. This lack of clarity about goals may have been the reason why the tutor quoted at the opening of the chapter saw her role as mundane. The goal of tutoring is to provide support for students' learning through taking advantage of the tutor's special position in the school. This special position allows the tutor to provide overall guidance and support related to all aspects of their lives. Sometimes this will be very specific support and guidance: for example, to Year 7 students as they transfer to secondary school, or to older students as they make choices and plans about their futures. For others this will be related to ensuring their readiness for learning: for example, with their organization of equipment, or with personal problems that are impacting on their learning.

We now explore further this idea that tutors occupy a special position in the school because it creates the potential for tutors to share knowledge about the students and their experience of school in a dialogue with the students and others about their learning. This dialogue takes place between teachers (including teachers in their role as tutor), between teachers and students and between students, and is most effective when it goes beyond the boundaries of the school to involve parents and others (see also Chapter 6).

The most common representation of the secondary school's structure places the tutor at the bottom of something that represents hierarchical relationships. Consider an alternative representation (Figure 4.1), which places the tutor at the hub of one set of relationships in the school. This diagram emphasizes the tutor's relationships within a complex multidimensional community. In reality the connections are much more complex than shown here because each group on the diagram also links with the others. However, here we focus on the tutor's connections and how they can be exploited to promote students' learning.

The tutor has three very valuable assets for helping tutees' learning when they are used in combination. First they have *knowledge of the school*, gained through:

- an overview of tutees' school experience;
- an overview of the planned curriculum;
- an understanding of the unplanned (or hidden) curriculum.

Second they have *knowledge of the students*, gained through:

- an overview of the progress and achievement of individual tutees;
- knowledge of the tutees over time;

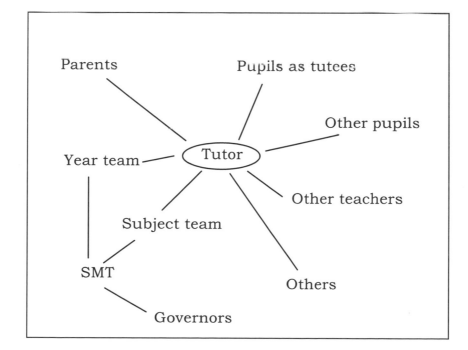

Figure 4.1   *The tutor's network*

- knowledge of the tutees' social circumstances.

Third, the tutors have the *potential to communicate* this knowledge to others because they:

- can encourage the group of tutees to share important knowledge about learning with each other;
- have access to communications with other teachers and adults in the school;
- have access to communications with parents and others in the community.

Not all tutors will have this complete experience, but the three aspects in combination – knowledge of the school, knowledge of the students and the potential to communicate this – can be exploited to help the tutees understand their own learning. How this may be done with the tutor group is explored next.

Supporting the learning of the tutor group

Many tutors see their role as primarily about working with individual students (Reynolds, 1995). Working with individuals is a very important part of the tutor's work and we explore focused learning conversations in the next chapter. The tutor who does not take advantage of the tutor group meeting together would be missing an important opportunity to explore their learning. The whole group context offers an opportunity for dialogue between tutor and students, and also between students. This dialogue is essential to co-constructivism in learning, as we have described in Chapters 1 and 2.

The tutorial session can be thought of as 'the laboratory for understanding about learning' (Marland and Rogers, 1997: 45). The laboratory is a place where resources are made available and shared in order that experimentation and discovery can take place. We suggest that in tutorial sessions the tutee and their learning are the focus of experiment and discovery. Few tutors will be able to devote all sessions to this, but we are suggesting the development of a planned programme to support young people's learning about learning (see below).

In working with the whole tutor group the tutor can bring an overview of the planned curriculum and their knowledge of the school and its resources. The tutees bring their experiences of the school and their different approaches to learning. The tutor can provide a relevant framework for their group to make connections between these elements. At times they may focus on the content of the learning in which the students are currently engaged, but at other times it will help the students to take a step back and look at learning more generally, that is, to develop meta-learning or learning about learning.

In this section we look at:

- connecting the curriculum;
- a programme for learning about learning;

- preparation for individual learning conversations;
- ensuring young people are ready for learning.

Connecting the curriculum

One of the functions that the tutor can perform with the group is to help the tutees make connections between apparently unconnected aspects of the curriculum. In school, the planned curriculum can often be experienced as incoherent and disconnected by the students. Hargreaves provided a particularly apt and brutal metaphor for students' perception of curriculum: 'Teachers see the curriculum as divided up into schemes of work, syllabuses, lessons, tasks. Each element is supposedly like a brick and, through schooling, the child builds the bricks into an edifice of the learnt curriculum, in reality, pupils stand amid a bomb-site of disconnected bricks and fragments' (Hargreaves, 1991: 31–2).

The tutor can help students find their way through the bomb-site and begin to understand the edifice in their teachers' minds. They do this by being alerted to connections in their learning. While individual subject teachers are able to provide guidance on learning in their own subject areas, working towards coherence of the curriculum overall is rarely supported structurally in the school: the forces are for fragmentation. The tutor can help young people see where the curriculum requires them to use related concepts or skills. For example, measurement and the presentation of statistical information recur in many subjects such as mathematics, technology and design, geography and history.[2] Many subjects require frameworks for extended written answers, and frameworks for doing this can be helpful across many subjects. Making these connections depends on the tutor having access to information about the curriculum.

Some schools have provided a programme that is organized around the idea of study skills. When the focus is on study skills, the skills and the learners are treated as if they are abstract, discrete, content-free and disembodied. Such programmes are unlikely to achieve their purposes in making the young person more effective at studying because they need to be linked into their practice. A more connected and holistic approach connects all aspects of learning: the skills, content, purpose, contexts and tasks. This connectivity is unlikely to be encouraged elsewhere in the school so the tutor has an important role here. It is important that there is no false separation between the teaching and tutoring functions of the school. So the focus on content and on meta-learning should be seen as connected activities.

A programme for learning about learning

Researchers interviewing children aged 10–14 found that 'many children seemed blissfully unaware that there *was* any procedure at all in learning. They did what was required of them – or rather what they thought the teacher wanted: teachers teach, and as a result children learn' (Nisbet and Shucksmith, 1984: 12). Many young people hold a similarly thin conception of learning, lacking insight into their own capacity to take charge of their own learning approaches. A programme to learn about learning, to develop the tutor group's meta-cognitive understandings can help them in this respect. Effective tutors, and tutor teams, are developing programmes of activities that help the group explore together issues such as:

- how we learn best;
- exploring experiences of learning;
- how students approach learning;
- different learning styles;
- different beliefs about success;
- looking at feelings in learning;
- what defences we have got against learning;
- learning in and out of school;
- reflective practice;
- thinking about the future.

Activities designed for young people to consider these questions can be found in *Learning about Learning* (Watkins et al., 2000).

In providing a learning about learning programme or curriculum the tutor focuses on the following aspects of learning:

- developing responsibility in the students' learning;
- developing and extending the students' language for talking about learning;
- developing useful frameworks and strategies for reviewing learning activities;
- paying attention to the transfer of these approaches to other areas of the curriculum.

Each of these is considered now in turn.

It is part of the tutor's role to help the tutees assume more responsibility for their own learning (Griffiths, 1995). In encouraging talk about learning and learning strategies, tutors are making it apparent to young people that there are choices about strategies, that alternative strategies are available to use and modify and that they can take responsibility for experimenting and taking risks. Tutors can encourage informal communication about learning within their tutor group, for example by setting up study, reading or homework groups. In Chapter 2 we gave examples of such arrangements, suggesting the dialogue in these groups needed to be characterized by engagement, openness and honesty in order to enhance responsibility in learning.

Young people need to develop the language in which to talk about their learning if they are to explore their experiences and consider different approaches. Making learning the object of attention is important in developing young people's capacities as learners. They need also to make learning an object of conversation, of dialogue. They need to explore the meanings of different activities in which they are involved: for example, analysis, description, brainstorming, synthesizing, evaluation, drafting, review, categorizing and rehearsal. Developing students' ability to be articulate about learning is an important aspect of meta-learning.

Effective learning requires reflection and tutors can help young people develop useful frameworks and strategies for reviewing learning activities. They can lead the tutor group through all four stages described in the *Do, Review, Learn and Apply* cycle in Chapter 1 to review their week or day or a particular lesson or task. Table 4.1 provides a framework for doing this.

Table 4.1   *A review framework for tutors*

DO

The tutor encourages and supports the tutees in active engagement in activities, tasks, processes.

REVIEW

The tutor facilitates the reflection, discussion and feedback and supports the emergence of new understandings and insights and the evaluation of learning strategies, especially in relation to:

their *purposes* in learning;
their *strategies* in learning;
the *effects* of their learning;
their *feelings* about the learning; and
the *context* of their learning.

LEARN

The tutor helps the tutor group to make learning explicit, to draw out insights and understandings that emerge in the review stage; the tutor supports comparisons and contrasts in present strategies and how they can be revised and developed from here.

APPLY

The tutor helps tutees plan future action differently in the light of new understanding, by promoting transfer of learning, planning of strategies for specific situations and contexts, and by setting new goals.

Source: Adapted from Watkins et al., 2000

In Table 4.1 we suggest that one of the tutor's functions is to promote transfer of learning. It is important that students can understand how to transfer learning about learning from one context to another, but it requires explicit attention. Claxton (2000) indicates that four elements are required for students to begin to understand that they can transfer some of these skills, strategies and approaches and practise them in different contexts. These contexts may include out of school learning. Tutors, therefore, need to be aware of these elements and include them in the programme for learning about learning.

1 A wide range of skills needs to be taught.
2 Learners need to be helped to recognize when a particular skill or approach is relevant.

3 Students' beliefs about learning need to be made explicit and if they are likely to block their learning the beliefs need to be challenged.
4 Opportunities need to be provided to reflect on the use of the particular skills, strategies and approaches.

In addition, it is powerful for students to see these skills, strategies and approaches modelled by their tutors and teachers (Claxton, 2000). The tutor can do this by seeing themselves as learners about their tutor groups, and investigating their learning across the school, and by sharing aspects of their own experiences of professional development, both content and at the meta-level of how they learned.

We have found that the time available for such programmes varies considerably from school to school. Tutorial sessions with the whole tutor group are usually allocated ten minutes or so, twice a day, and perhaps one tutorial lesson a week. Even in schools where the tutor groups only meet briefly the tutor can engage their group in a programme such as we suggest. In one school the tutors introduce a series of short 'Start of Day' activities that focus students on learning before the subject timetable begins and they are designed to be explicit about their learning. In other schools that have one tutorial lesson a week we have found learning about learning included in the tutorial programmes. In some schools this is integrated into the PSHE programme and taught by tutors or others.

Preparation for individual learning conversations

In the next chapter we describe how individual learning conversations need preparation by the students if they are to be effective. In particular, students need to be able to talk about their learning, to be familiar with the language to describe their strategies, feelings, effects and blocks. This preparation can be done as a group activity during a learning programme.

Ensuring young people are ready for learning

There are also the mundane aspects to the tutor's support for learning. Ensuring that the students are well organized and ready for learning can appear repetitive and unproductive: giving out timetables, signing homework diaries, checking equipment, resolving and quieting small-scale conflicts. Some tutors have used specific techniques such as meditation and Circle Time to help students prepare for learning. Both these strategies are described in Chapter 9. Many students find it useful to have support from someone in ensuring they are ready for learning.

The skills required by the tutor to engage in a learning curriculum are not different in essence from those of the subject teacher, or those behaviours which students regularly say they welcome in good teachers. In Chapter 2 we reported that a Year 8 class unanimously voted for 'someone who listens' as 'quality number one' for an ideal teacher (Sullivan, 2000). They also wanted someone who explains clearly and someone 'who allows us our own opinions' (Sullivan, 2000: 79–80). When we asked teachers to identify the key tutoring skills, they also started with listening, and added approachability, good communications skills, consistency and fairness, good organization, a knowledge of sources of support and imagination.[3]

In this part of the chapter we suggest that the most effective learning curriculum for a tutor group will be one informed by the tutor's knowledge of their tutees' progress across the planned curriculum and in all their school activities. It will also connect the tutees' experiences in subject lessons and inform the work of other teachers. This focus on the students and their learning needs to be supported by the tutor's knowledge of their tutor group's experiences within the context of the school and their homes. This brings us to the role of the tutor in ensuring effective communication between students and their teachers and parents about their learning.

Communicating with other teachers

Let us now turn to how the tutor can support learning through combining their special position in their network with the knowledge they have of the students and the school. Some teachers are uncomfortable with the suggestion that the tutor can provide them with information to adapt their teaching. They feel that teachers should not be told how to teach, but such information can help them take more account of how the students are learning. We now look at some ways in which this can happen.

Information provider

There may be information that the tutor can communicate to the teacher, to help the teacher in their work. Tutors are familiar with the need to give subject teachers some kinds of personal information about their tutees that affect their learning (such as a bereavement or a hearing difficulty, for example). Other information may relate to learning strategies being attempted by the students, to effective learning relationships within the group, or to some forthcoming aspect of the curriculum which links with other subject areas.

The tutor might also help the tutee make use of information from their subject teacher, especially in relation to feedback on assignments. Research studies have highlighted the importance of feedback, not marks or grades, but feedback that gives each student specific guidance on what is going well and how to improve (Askew, 2000; Black and Wiliam, 1998).

Advocate

The tutor may act as advocate for the students, placing the learning entitlement of the students at the heart of the communication with other teachers.

An obvious example would be to promote provision for a student with special educational needs, but the principles that operate for Individual Education Plans (IEPs) can be applied to all students. Students may have been working on action planning, and aspects of the plan will need communicating to the subject teachers. A tutor may need to represent the opinion or position of a student in a dispute with a teacher.

Collaboration

The teacher and tutor may work together to support the group's learning. For example, in one school where each class had a museum visit every year, their tutor accompanied the history class to explore the Egyptian collection. Both history teacher and tutor made use of the experience in their subsequent lessons, especially as the tutor was also the form's drama teacher. The shared experience helped both teacher and tutor in future discussions about the members of the group and their learning.

Chairing tutor group team discussions

In another school, the tutor calls together the teachers of the tutor group, once a term, to discuss their progress. These meetings are specifically to look at their learning and not to discuss problem students or behaviours that cause concern. There was another forum for this. In Chapter 3, Alison Heap refers to the value of such a meeting for Danijel, the refugee experiencing difficulties in his new school. These meetings serve a similar purpose to the Year Learning Teams described in Chapter 7.

Mediator

The tutor sometimes needs to act as a mediator. For example, many schools find that students complain when all their subject deadlines arrive at the same time, and tutors can negotiate more achievable deadlines with the teachers. In Tony Fraser's example of individual tutoring (see Chapter 5), the tutors sometimes paved the way for a difficult conversation between the subject teacher and student, giving the student impetus and confidence.

All this depends upon information being available to the tutor, and communications between teachers being fluid and flexible. This can be problematic in large secondary schools, or where the site does not encourage frequent meetings. Some schools are experimenting with e-mail or voice mail for their teachers, to reduce the dependence on paper communication. The student must also be linked into this network, and it can be especially useful if they can share e-mail and other conversations. It also depends on a climate of shared responsibility for the learning of the students. In this kind of school talk of the pastoral–curricular divide is minimal (see Chapter 7).

Communicating with families

We know that parents are very influential in young people's attitudes, motivation, modelling and aspirations. We also know that many students turn to members of their family for help when they meet a learning block.[4] Families are also more significant than teachers in discussions about subject choices and careers (Keys and Fernandes, 1993).[5]

Tutors are in a position to be a valuable source of guidance for families, through dialogue with parents about the family's aspirations for the student, about how to support students with homework and at difficult times (such as preparation for examinations, or choosing courses and planning post-school learning). A systematic programme of tutor and family meetings throughout the year can help this communication. It is important for students to be present to give their own perspective to the discussions.

Tutors may also be helpful in ensuring the teachers have access to important information from the parents and family relevant to the young people's learning. Engaging in such dialogues with families is a theme we explore further in Chapter 6.

School issues in realizing effective tutoring for learning

The role of tutor is often poorly defined. The purposes and processes of the role can be neglected and remain inexplicit and hidden or be diverted into some of the distortions to which pastoral care is prone. Membership of a pastoral team can be very useful for clarifying the role and supporting individual teachers in their professional development as tutors (see Chapter 7).

Tutors often feel ill-prepared for many aspects of their role. They complain that little attention was paid to it in their initial teacher education and that professional development of tutors has been neglected in favour of other aspects of the teacher's work in the last decade. This may be improving as a result of more school-centred professional development, of experienced teachers mentoring beginning teachers and newly qualified teachers and of the introduction of statutory training days (Best, 1999). It remains true that: 'the UK education system has always spoken of the importance of the role [of tutor], but less often defined it or prepared teachers for it' (Marland and Rogers, 1997: 11). The resources required for professional development of tutors are simple to state, but harder to provide as the main one is time. Time is necessary for the tutors to work with groups, with individuals and to communicate with others. Tutors also need the support of teams (see Chapter 7), and formal and informal professional development opportunities (Griffiths, 1995).

There are likely to be a number of other factors that work against tutors and their teams developing the kinds of strategies suggested above, despite evidence that they can be effective. Solutions will need to be found within each institution, but they are likely to include some of the following:

- provision of symbolic support for the tutor, especially by the headteacher and pastoral team leaders;

- provision of structures to foster collaboration (e.g. co-tutoring, effective communications, tutor team meetings);
- ensuring continuous professional development;
- establishing planning, monitoring, review and evaluation procedures for tutors and their teams;
- continuous dialogue in the school about the purposes of tutoring, what it means to be a tutor, and effective tutorial practices;
- continuous dialogue in the school about learning and how it can be enhanced.

The rewards for the form tutor are huge, in providing a most satisfactory relationship with a whole group of young people and the satisfaction of seeing them become effective learners. Some of these suggestions are beyond the means of individual tutors. The tutor's role in supporting students' learning would be immensely enhanced if the school procedures mirrored learning strategies and adopted the approach of a learning community (see Chapter 9). These would be evident in such processes as the learning policy, problem-solving strategies, review procedures, teamwork and staff development.

Conclusion

Evidence from research indicates that an emphasis on tutoring is effective in promoting learning. Some schools appear to be particularly successful in maintaining the motivation of their students beyond their first year in secondary school. A report from Keele University identified three strategies used by those schools.

1 They developed effective differentiation in the classroom.
2 They invested time in tutorial work.
3 They valued out-of-school activities (Barber and Graham, 1994).

The report indicated that the tutorial system was the most effective of these three strategies in promoting student motivation: 'It might be expected that school managements would get the best return in increased pupil satisfaction by investing in differentiation. On the evidence of our small sample, however, investment of time and energy in the tutorial system appears to be even more effective' (Barber and Graham, 1994: 5).

Developing effective tutoring to support learning presents problems that may be largely in the hands of those who decide school policy, but the tutor can make a significant contribution to students' learning without waiting for structural alterations. Tutors have two key assets: their own special position in the school and the opportunity to focus on the group's learning in ways that connect these experiences. Individually these are important resources, but together these are powerful resources for creating a laboratory for learning for every student.

We began this chapter by quoting a rather limited view of tutoring offered during a staff development day. Later on that day the same person suggested that one of the key functions for tutors in supporting students' learning is to act as a model of a learner. They can be explicit about their own learning approaches, learning blocks, favoured conditions, enthusiasms, forms of co-operation and so forth. This requires reflection on their own learning. We hope this chapter has contributed to the continued learning of the tutor by providing more frameworks and strategies for them to try, review, learn from and adapt again.

Notes

1 A version of this chapter was originally published in *Pastoral Care in Education*, as 'Tutors and Students' Learning or Why do School have Tutors?' (Lodge, 2000a).
2 A useful exercise in monitoring the curriculum for a tutor is to review the number of times in their first week in secondary school that students are asked to draw maps of their bedrooms: in mathematics to look at scale, in geography to consider the concepts of plans and scale, in French to practise their vocabulary, in PSHE to explore contexts for homework and so forth. The value of such repetition could be reviewed.
3 We are grateful to the participants at a NAPCE workshop, 'Becoming a Form Tutor', for extending our understanding of a number of points in this chapter.
4 Rescarch based on interviews and questionnaires reveals that up to 50 per cent of students turn to a member of their family for help when they get stuck at school. A large group never consider asking a teacher (Lodge, 2000b).
5 Year 9 students were asked: Do you talk to your form tutor about your career plans?

Often	4.5%
Sometimes	28.8%
Hardly	52.5%
N/a	14.1%

And: Do you talk to your parents about your career plans?

Often	44.9%
Sometimes	44.1%
Hardly	6.8%
N/a	4.1%

Further reading

Best, R., Lang, P., Lodge, C. and Watkins, C. (eds) (1995) *Pastoral Care and Personal-Social Education: Entitlement and Provision*. London: Cassell.

Marland, M. and Rogers, R. (1997) *The Art of the Tutor: Developing your Role in the Secondary School*. London: David Fulton.

5
Learning Conversations[1]

In this chapter we examine an important aspect of supporting young people's learning – individual learning conversations, sometimes called mentoring or academic tutoring.

Here we use 'tutoring' to refer to a structured conversation between tutor and tutee with an explicit focus on learning. It is not necessarily a role of the form tutor only – we see tutoring as a function that can be undertaken by a number of different people. We argue for an approach that structures the learning conversation around the *Do, Review, Learn and Apply* cycle of learning that we refer to throughout this book.

Tutoring is not a new concept, it has been happening for a long time, both formally and informally. There is no one accepted term: it is called academic tutoring, mentoring, tutorial interviews, personal tutoring, academic tracking, academic review, tutorial reviews, achievement target setting, work reviews, monitoring and other combinations of these terms. What might be new for some teachers is the more structured and planned approach to individual conversations with young people that we are suggesting, as opposed to informal 'chats'. We argue the most effective forms of conversations are those which mirror either the constructivist or the co-constructivist approach to learning (see Chapter 1). In the constructivist approach the 'tutor' acts as a facilitator, the 'tutee' has responsibility for their learning and the process is about making meaning. In the co-constructivist approach learning is seen as a dialogue.

In this chapter we consider the ways in which teachers and other 'tutors' in schools develop tutoring practices, develop their rationales and consider links with learning. We examine learner preparation and a way of structuring learning conversations to make them more effective. To illustrate some of the themes we include a case study showing how a tutoring process was evaluated in one school and what was learned from young people about effective and not so effective tutoring experiences. We discuss some important issues emerging from the case study including finding time for tutoring, teachers' professional development and how tutoring might be integrated with other aspects of school life to make young people's experiences of learning more coherent.

The development of tutoring practices

Our work with teachers around the country indicates that more and more schools are investing time and other resources in tutoring. From our research we have found that some schools started with a particular target group (for example, a year group, boys, students who are on the borderline for GCSE grade C/D). We have noted a trend towards involving *all* pupils as schools come to see the value of individual learning conversations. We also found that in some schools all teachers are involved in tutoring, whereas in others the role of tutor falls to either the form tutors, senior managers, mentors, careers advisers or other adults not on the school staff. For example, the Excellence in Cities initiative uses learning mentors who may not be teachers. (Also see Chapter 6 where we suggest parents and others in the community can act as tutors.)

It is useful to consider the underpinning rationale for tutoring in your school, its history and its implementation. For example, what is the process called? Is it formal or informal, planned or unplanned? Is there a school policy on individual tutoring or do some tutors fit individual tutoring in when they are with their tutor group? Which students are targeted? Which members of staff or other adults are involved? When does tutoring happen and how often? Answers to these sorts of questions may illuminate your school's rationale.

Rationales for tutoring

In our work with teachers we have found that schools sometimes introduce individual tutoring based on an unexamined assumption, such as, it may raise the young person's self-esteem, without clarifying their understanding of the links between self esteem and learning. Tutors need to clarify purposes, processes and goals for tutoring. In practice this may mean some experiences of tutoring are less effective than others. Given the amount of time this process may take, it is important that individual learning conversations are worthwhile. Considering the different rationales underpinning individual tutoring helps clarify how learning conversations might be made more effective in helping young people become more effective learners.

There may be differences in perceptions among teachers and young people about the purposes of tutoring. In a research study carried out by Val Dagley at Cromer High School in Norfolk involving 17 teachers and 101 students she found a wide variety of perceptions and practices:

> In spite of the Headteacher's statement that the aim of the interviews was to set targets and to raise standards, others in the school had different views about the purposes of the interviews. The majority of the *students* thought that they were to enable tutor monitoring and control: 'to see how you are getting on'; 'to keep you on track'; 'to see what we are up to'. As far as *tutors* were concerned, problem solving was the prominent concern, although the Head of Upper School did say in a memo that the interviews should aim to 'increase the personal effectiveness of students so that they can solve their own problems'. (Dagley, 2000)

Such differences in perceptions about tutoring are important to make explicit in the school both with teachers and with young people, as individual perceptions will determine responses to tutoring. The tutor and tutee need to agree goals at the start of the conversation. The effectiveness of the practice across the school will depend on a shared understanding of goals and practices, responsibilities and outcomes.

We now discuss a number of different views about individual tutoring to develop an argument for a specific focus on learning. We include nine statements that we have heard teachers say when they describe why they think tutoring works. When reading these statements consider your responses:

1 It gives the pupils more personal attention.
2 It makes pupils work harder.
3 The pupils can make connections between different aspects of the curriculum.
4 It gives pupils time to reflect.
5 It helps pupils be strategic about examinations.
6 It helps pupils develop more strategies and approaches to learning.
7 The pupils are given targets by their teachers.
8 It allows pupils a greater sense of control and responsibility for their achievement.
9 It helps pupils learn more about their own learning.

We address each of these statements to argue for tutoring as a specific occasion for a learning conversation to help *pupils learn more about their own learning* (statement 9).

Young people and their tutors may value time together in which pupils get *more personal attention* (statement 1). However, in tutoring time we question the value of personal attention if it is not focused on the tutee's learning. In tutoring if personal attention alone is all they are getting it may be an inefficient and expensive use of time. If there is a focus on learning while they are getting personal attention, the time is used more effectively.

Some tutors may consider that giving pupils more personal attention will foster the development of relationships between them. While we do not underestimate the importance of personal relationships between tutee and tutor, in tutoring time we feel that a focus on learning itself may be of more help to the learner. We question using tutoring time for this; relationships in schools are not an end in themselves. Personal attention and the development of relationships can happen on different sorts of occasions.

The suggestion of *working harder* (statement 2) is one we hear both young people and teachers making. Working harder may be a trap for students as they may repeat mistakes rather then reflect, learn, adapt and move on. We suggest changing the language from working harder to *learning effectively* as this language changes the young people's and teachers' conceptions of what young people are doing in school. Helping young people learn effectively is the most important goal of tutoring (see Chapter 4).

Statements 3, 4, 5 and 6 support students' learning but only in part. Statement 3 refers to *making connections between different aspects of the curriculum*. We see this as important in tutoring providing tutees are helped to make connections about their learning. For example, what are they noticing about when learning works best and when learning is difficult. By focusing attention on the learning it helps tutees become more aware of what helps and hinders their learning and what they might do to address any difficulties they encounter. This is a way of giving tutees responsibility for their actions.

Time to reflect (statement 4) is necessary for learning but reflection alone does not result in learning. As we see from the *Do, Review, Learn and Apply* cycle (see Chapter 1) there needs to be a specific focus on learning and on applying that learning in order to bring about effective change. Reflection alone may result in the situation staying the same. We argue effective learning requires change. Statements 5, *it helps pupils be strategic about examinations*, and 6, *it helps pupils develop more strategies and approaches to learning*, are important but these two may not bring about change in learning either.

Young people need to be responsible for their own decisions to become effective learners so *tutors giving targets to students* (statement 7) is unhelpful. Val Dagley's research indicates that students are positive about target-setting only when they set them for themselves. As one student said: 'The tutor reminded me to set targets and encouraged me to meet them.' Whereas another student commented: 'I feel embarrassed, she goes on and on and decides on my target even if I don't need to work on that' (Dagley, 2000). Targets need to focus on learning rather than performance (see Chapter 1 where we discuss the difference between 'learning orientation' and 'performance orientation') and be identified by young people themselves. Later in the chapter we examine the difference between a learning target and a performance target.

A sense of control and responsibility for their achievement is seen in statement 8, but this refers only to achievement. Such an approach may not address learning explicitly and a focus on achievement may reinforce performance rather than learning.

We argue the most effective tutoring experiences are those that focus explicitly on learning (statement 9 *it helps pupils learn more about their own learning*). A focus on learning about learning is a meta-learning process (see Chapter 1) and this, we argue, has the most impact. The focus on their own learning is not an empty discussion; it does relate to the content of the learning.

This rationale for tutoring underpins the development of increasing students' own understanding of their learning and of themselves as learners. This contrasts with the view of the Year 11 student we quoted in the Introduction to this book: 'It's not that I haven't learnt much. It's just that I don't really understand what I am doing' (Harris et al., 1995: 253).

Later in the chapter we provide a structure for the tutorial which helps tutors and tutees focus on learning.

The relation between tutoring and models of learning

Effective tutoring, in our view, addresses the problem identified by this Year 11 student, by having an explicit focus on learning about learning, increasing student engagement and developing more positive feelings about learning. This approach increases a sense of ownership and responsibility by the learner. This approach to tutoring matches the characteristics of the constructivist model of learning, for example, reflection, critical investigation, analysis, interpretation and reorganization of knowledge (see Chapter 1). The tutor encourages the tutee to reflect, review their learning within a particular context and relate it to previous experiences and understandings; the emphasis is on learning not on performance.

An emphasis on performance would be a characteristic of the reception model of learning. If tutoring were based on the reception model, statement 7 *the pupils are given targets by their teachers* would apply. In this scenario the tutor would tell the student what to do. This approach is less likely to be successful as the tutees have less commitment to the targets if they have not identified the targets for themselves. Target setting may not need one-to-one conversations. This process could be done as a whole class where young people may help each other to identify learning targets for themselves.

Bullock and Wikeley suggest that the emphasis on target-setting has appeared to encourage the misconception that setting targets is equivalent to learning. Bullock and Wikeley's research shows that learning is not the same as target-setting:

> Students regard a target as a task for completion and may or may not achieve it; and may or may not learn from it. In general terms, students have not yet considered the nature of learning nor identified the learning skills that could be practised, and they did not understand that learning is both active and reflective. (Bullock and Wikeley, 2000: 6)

Target-setting with peers within form tutor periods, for example, allows opportunities for young people to learn together about different aspects of their learning and how target setting can support learning.

We have heard of few examples where tutoring is based on the co-constructivist model. In this approach tutoring is seen differently. For example, we draw on our own experiences as adults working with peers. We ask teachers to review an aspect of their work, for example, a meeting with parents or a professional development workshop they organized.

First, peers tutor each other, taking it in turns to be the 'tutor' and 'tutee'. This has the advantage of both developing the skills of both roles. Second, tutoring is seen as a dialogue where both, or even a small group, talk together in an equal relationship about their learning. We illustrate this in Chapter 6 where we examine the ways in which young people and their parents learn together round the kitchen table. This is not a 'chat', as it has purpose, focus and direction. This form of dialogue has the advantage of spontaneity and the possibility of developing insights by being engaged in developing meaning together. The goal in co-constructivist tutoring is to help people develop skills to support others' learning. This goal illustrates that co-constructivism is not just about the activity, but relates also to supportive roles, explicit group dynamics and relationships.

Tutoring, in a co-constructivist approach may work more effectively as there is not an imbalance in power; there is 'relational responsibility' (McNamee and Gergen, 1999). For example, peers may be able to be more honest, open and be able to give each other support on a more regular basis than a teacher could offer a young person. Social and emotional aspects are crucial in a co-constructivist approach.

The links between tutoring and learning

In the discussion above, important features emerge in tutoring to do with the processes of reviewing, learning and applying involved. These processes link with the model of learning introduced in Chapter 1 (see Figure 5.1).

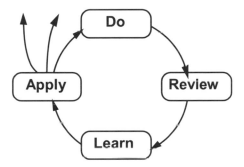

Figure 5.1   *A learning cycle* (Dennison and Kirk, 1990)

In tutoring conversations this model can be applied as a structure when the tutor (either adult or peer) supports the tutee through the different stages:

- reviewing experiences;
- abstracting the meaning from this;
- planning the next steps;
- being involved in further activity.

The conversation may focus on the subject matter of students' learning, but will be most effective when it also involves an awareness of their learning strategies, blocks to learning, feelings about their learning, the context and their purposes – that is, an understanding of their own learning. We call this meta-learning (see Chapter 1). The most effective conversations are explicit about these aspects of learning.

Table 5.1 outlines a structure we have devised to illustrate the stages in a learning conversation, focusing on the review, learn and apply aspects of the

Table 5.1 *Stages in a tutorial learning conversation*

Stage of learning conversation	Skills for tutors	Examples of tutor prompts
• Reviewing: exploring the situation	– Active listening – Asking open questions – Being non-judgemental	What's going well? And not so well . . .[1] How do you feel about this?
• Learning: identifying new insights and understandings	– Empathizing – Reflecting back – Sharing insights	How do you make sense of what's happening? New insights you have gained are ...[1] Are you noticing any patterns in your learning? What have you noticed about what helps your learning and what blocks it?
• Applying: taking the learning forward	– Establishing clear, negotiated goals – Supporting planning and target-setting (targets need to be learning targets rather than performance targets, see below)	Your next steps will be ...[1] What and who do you need to help you? If you get stuck you will talk to . . .[1] When will the next review be most helpful?
• Review of the learning conversation: a meta-learning level. Its purpose is to stand back from the conversation and consider how it helped or hindered learning	Skills at this stage are the same as those in the earlier review stage: – Active listening – Asking open questions – Being non-judgemental	• What did you notice about today's tutorial? • In what ways did you find it effective? • Describe the changes in your feelings during the tutorial. • In what ways are you finding talking about your learning more effective? • Is there anything you are noticing about my role that is helping or hindering your learning?

1 The tutor does not complete this sentence but encourages the student to do so. It is a prompt.

learning cycle. We have identified in Table 5.1 the skills used by tutors and some examples of tutor prompts.

The example prompts we have included in Table 5.1 are non-specific. For that reason they may look more sophisticated than they might be in practice as prompts at the 'learning stage' connect with what emerges from the 'reviewing stage' of the conversation. The language may be unfamiliar. But when it is related to content it becomes more accessible. For learning to be effective language needs to become richer as this will extend the learners' thinking and understanding. This underscores the value of student preparation that we discuss later in the chapter.

In Table 5.2 we distinguish between learning targets and performance targets. A learning target has an emphasis on learning and a performance target has an emphasis on performance. This distinction can be demonstrated in the following example.

Table 5.2 *The difference between a performance target and learning target*

Performance target	Learning target
Achieving a C grade in Mathematics GCSE.	Understanding the learning strategies necessary to achieve a grade C in Mathematics GCSE.

In Chapter 1 we argue the case for an emphasis on learning rather than performance.

In Table 5.1 we have included a review of the learning conversation. This review allows both the young person and the tutor to learn about the process of tutoring. This review is carried out at a meta-learning level, that is to say, the focus is on the learning itself. This is an important focus as we gather from an evaluation of Personal Learning Planning that while both tutees and tutors enjoyed the experience of individual tutoring, it seemed that both failed to make the most out of the process:

> Pupils were not able to make the link with learning about learning. Tutors discovered interesting information about their pupils, but in general, missed the opportunity to explore the dynamics of individual pupil learning. A one-to-one discussion with students is clearly a learning opportunity for teachers, as well as students. (Bullock and Wikeley, 2000: 5)

We believe that the emphasis on learning is the most effective use of tutoring time as it makes an explicit link with learning about learning. The review of the learning conversation provides an opportunity for young people to give feedback to their tutors. This is a way in which the occasion can become a learning opportunity for the tutors.

The tutor's role

The tutor's role (whether teacher, learning mentor, peer, parent or other) is to structure the learning conversation by moving the student through the stages; the order of prompts encourages this (see Table 5.1). The structure ensures reflection on the activity at the outset, moving on to learning from the experiences, planning future action and strategies and finally reflecting at a meta-learning level. In this way the conversation follows a complete cycle of learning.

There are some important points to note about the conversation. For example, questions and prompts should be open-ended, inviting exploration; relentless questioning can be off-putting. There should be time to allow for thinking and there may be some periods of silence.

The tutor may not be the main source of ideas for future strategies so the learner can be encouraged to:

- use their imagination – for example, *what might you do? What might a friend advise you to do?*
- think of other credible people – for example, *do you know of anyone who seems to be handling this sort of problem well? What might X do?*
- think as a third party – for example, *if you were advising a friend about this, what could help them achieve their goal?*
- anticipate – for example, *what will help me succeed or hinder me? How might others respond?* (Watkins and Butcher, 1995)

Helping someone review their progress and achievement requires the skills of active listening and appropriate questioning or prompting. Active listening requires respect, sincerity and genuineness. It involves paraphrasing, prompting and probing. It needs judgement about the use of open, closed and leading questions and when to move forward. Although the tutor often speaks very little, they will be concentrating hard on listening, checking their physical responses, monitoring the progress of the review and deciding when to move on.

The learners' contributions grow as they develop a shared language with which to describe their learning through talking about learning with each other and with teachers. In the case study that follows, students said the processes of tutoring subsequently helped them talk to their subject teachers as it enriched their language.

Tutoring: a case study

We now look at a case study that illuminates some of the issues we have raised and provides research evidence to suggest that tutoring can help young people's learning and achievement. We should point out that this case study looks specifically at a tutoring initiative designed to improve GCSE grades and therefore stresses performance rather than learning *per se*.

Case study   Pupils' perceptions of a system of individual academic tutoring at Key Stage 4 and its effects: one school's experience
Tony Fraser

Introduction

What did we do right? (Anonymous teacher, 1998)

Helena Romanes School is a mixed comprehensive school of over 1,300 pupils aged between 11 and 18 in 'semi-rural' Essex. In November 1999 the school was listed as one of the top 50 most improved schools in England and Wales (Guardian, 1999) because 63 per cent of our Year 11 pupils had gained 5 or more GCSE passes at Grades A* to C (the government-approved yard-stick of success) compared with a score of 44 per cent in 1996.

There were many initiatives that contributed to a process of school improve-ment during the 1990s, a period in which attendance rates and A level results in the school both improved markedly. However the cohort of pupils who gained the real breakthrough in GCSE results in 1998 (59 per cent gaining five or more Grades A* to C) was the first to experience Academic Tutoring. Amidst the celebrations we began to ask – was it the 'magic bullet' that had sparked this improvement?

Individual Academic Tutoring at Helena Romanes School

> It makes being a tutor worthwhile. (Experienced form tutor, 1999)

We adopted a system of Academic Tutoring very similar to that used in the London Borough of Sutton and publicised by Betterton and Nash (1996). Individual interviews of approximately 15 minutes duration between every pupil and his or her form tutor lie at the heart of the process. These interviews happen twice a year. The purpose of the interview is to review progress and agree targets for improvement. It was clear from the outset that the provision of sufficient time would be crucial to the success of Academic Tutoring. The school invested in the system by

(i) increasing the number of Year 10 form tutors, thus reducing the average number of pupils per tutor and making the process more manageable.
(ii) releasing tutors from their timetable on two days in the school year to conduct interviews with their tutees (sometimes accompanied by par-ents). INSET [in-service training] time was set aside beforehand to pro-vide tutors with guidance in conducting interviews.

The purpose of the Review Days was to ensure 'quality time' for tutors and all their tutees in addition to existing opportunities for discussing progress.

The research – why and how

> What pupils say about teaching, learning and schooling is . . . perhaps the most important foundation for thinking about ways of improving schools. (Rudduck et al., 1996: 1)

It is disappointing to note that Stoll and Smith (1997) reported that most schools did not see pupil involvement as essential or important in making schools more effective. In addition, little on the subject of Academic Tutoring or similar processes appears in 'the literature' and then seldom from the pupil's viewpoint. This encouraged me to investigate students' perceptions of Academic Tutoring.

In April 1999 all available members (86 per cent overall) of three year groups in the school were surveyed by questionnaire. The groups chosen were Year 12, whose members had completed two years of Academic Tutoring, Year 10 (in the first year of the process) and Year 9, who were about to commence it. Most questions were closed, using a 7 point Likert scale, e.g.

How well do you think your tutor knows/knew your standard of work and progress?	Very well								Not at all well

Responses were scored from 7 to 1, with high scores representing positive answers (e.g. 'very well' in the above example).

A few more open-ended questions, such as 'Please write down any suggestions you have for improving Academic Tutoring in this school' were also included. Respondents were divided, by means of their average scores on age-standardized Cognitive Ability Tests, into three bands of approximately equal size and identified only by gender and this ability grouping.

The results

1 Attitudes to Academic Tutoring and target-setting

Responses from Year 10 and Year 12 pupils revealed that the actual processes of Academic Tutoring and recording their own personal targets were not very popular (mean scores for both activities were below the neutral point). However over 70 per cent of these pupils expressed no particular dislike of any aspect of Academic Tutoring and when they were asked to suggest improvements, requests for longer or more frequent interviews outnumbered all other suggestions. Over one-third of all pupils surveyed would find this desirable, with the idea more popular with girls (38 per cent) than with boys (28 per cent).

Pupils' perceptions of the beneficial effects of Academic Tutoring were more positive and yielded significant differences, both by gender and between ability groupings. Boys were generally more inclined to say that Academic Tutoring had increased their confidence in terms of tackling GCSE and more likely to feel that it had helped their exam results. This resonates with Bullock and Wikeley's (1999) finding that the benefits of personal learning plans were more widespread for boys than for girls. The most striking differences occurred when ability groupings were considered, with pupils in the low ability group demonstrating the greatest faith in Academic Tutoring. For instance, responses to the question below are shown in Figure 5.2.

Has/did Academic Tutoring made it easier for you to talk to your *subject* teachers about your progress?	Yes, a lot easier								No not at all

Similarly lower ability pupils have the greatest faith in Academic Tutoring to improve their examination performance and increase their confidence about doing well at GCSE whilst high ability pupils have the least and tend to report little or no effect on their confidence. The former group also tended to respond

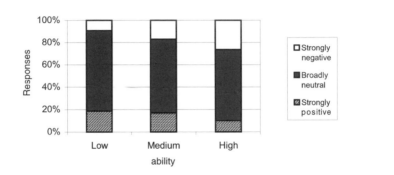

Figure 5.2 *Ability groupings' responses*

most positively to the question although we can take some encouragement that overall levels of response to this question were positive, with mean scores in all year groups around 4.5.

| How much does it help you to have targets to work towards? | A lot | | | | | | | | Not at all |

Year 9 pupils' expectations of Academic Tutoring were rather more positive (mean score = 4.32) and they tend to enjoy recording their targets more, perhaps because, unlike their elders, this is something they have done throughout their secondary school careers. It is interesting to note that some of them believed that although they would not like the process it would help them to achieve better GCSE results!

2 Self-knowledge and attitudes to learning

In these areas scores were high throughout, with all mean scores above 5 and some nearer to 6. Any differences seem to reinforce the findings noted earlier. For instance boys' responses to the question were more positive than those of girls in all three year groups, especially Year 12, who were asked to comment retrospectively on their work in Year 11.

| How clear are/were you about what you need(ed) to do to improve your grades? | Very clear | | | | | | | | Not at all clear |

Increasing certainty, with age, about their strengths in schoolwork was also more marked for boys than for girls. Similar patterns emerged in responses to two 'paired' questions examining pupils' reported level of interest in their courses at the time and expected level in the following year. Hardly surprisingly, Year 9 pupils, having just chosen GCSE courses, were the most likely to reply optimistically (see Figure 5.3), but at a time when boys' lack of motivation is a cause of concern, the results illustrated in Figure 5.4 make interesting reading.

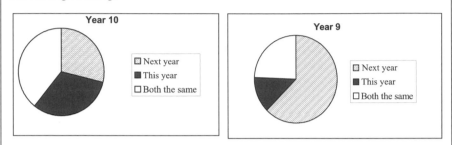

Figure 5.3   *Which courses are/will be more interesting?*

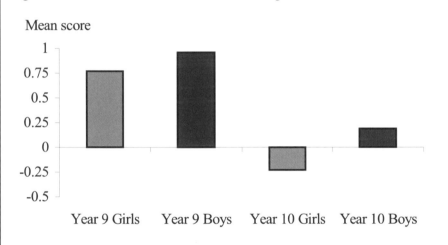

Figure 5.4   *Next year's courses vs this year's courses*

The gains observed may be merely a function of later maturing in adolescent boys but the proposition that some process experienced during Years 10 and 11 (possibly Academic Tutoring) bolsters our male pupils' interest and confidence in their work cannot be ruled out.

In Year 9 certainty about current progress and academic strengths rises significantly with increasing ability. Reduced differences in later years support the finding that less able pupils are more likely to perceive Academic Tutoring as beneficial. In contrast high ability pupils in all years seem to be the least certain about general strategies to obtain further improvement. This may stem from their receiving less advice from teachers than students who are achieving less well. However, high-ability pupils do outscore low attainers in terms of knowing which areas of their work need improvement. It can be argued that they are perhaps more astute in analysing their work in different subjects and pinpointing for themselves the specific areas in need of attention.

3 Talking to teachers

> I felt kind of good because it felt as if people actually cared about how well I did. (Boy, Year 12)

The one-to-one interview is central to the Academic Tutoring process and for many pupils the opportunity to discuss achievements and strategies for further improvement has been rewarding, an effect noted by Broadfoot et al. (1988) and Pole (1993) in their evaluations of Records of Achievement. Unfortunately other pupils have seen it as merely 'useless chat' (Year 10 pupil).

In general pupils in Years 10 and 12 seemed to find talking to their tutors individually about their progress quite easy (mean scores were 4.97 and 4.96 respectively) but the question

Who talks/talked most when you are/were discussing your progress with your tutor?	I do/did							My tutor does/did

revealed a more marked perception of tutor-dominated discussion in Year 10, especially amongst boys in that year group. Questionnaires were grouped, anonymously, by tutor group and it is clear that the identity/personality of the tutor was a major factor in these results. In addition there is some evidence of correlation between high levels of tutor domination in interviews and pupils' lack of belief in the benefits of Academic Tutoring.

All respondents were asked how easy they found it to talk to subject teachers about their work (Year 12 pupils were asked to look back to Year 11). Year 9 pupils reported much greater difficulty than other students did. Whether such increased facility with age is the product of maturation or Academic Tutoring cannot be determined. However it is interesting to note that Year 12 pupils are more likely than those in Year 10 to ascribe it to involvement in the latter process, a result that could be due to their greater experience of Academic Tutoring and the advantage of hindsight.

Responses to the open-ended question 'What do you consider should be the most important part of your tutor's job in Years 10 and 11?' reflect how far some schools have progressed in the past decade. In Kitteringham's survey (1987), where students were asked to rank five aspects of the form tutor's job in order of importance, administrative activity (such as taking the register) ranked second overall. In my case study such activity received no mentions in Year 9 and very few in Years 10 and 12. The tutor's role in the school has developed considerably over recent years and Year 9 pupils should have experienced this aspect of the tutor's work since their first arrival in the school. It is therefore not surprising that their expectations of tutors in Key Stage 4 are similar to pupils who have already experienced Academic Tutoring.

Conclusions and recommendations

> A good school does not emerge like pre-packed frozen dinner stuck for 15 seconds in a radar range; it develops from the slow simmering of carefully blended ingredients. (Sizer, 1985: 22)

I believe that, properly used, Academic Tutoring has an important part to play in education, as can be seen by our experience at Helena Romanes School. Whilst it is dangerous to read too much into the results of research carried out at one school at a single point in time, the consistency of many of my results with those of other similar studies (e.g. Bullock & Wikeley, 1999; Bullock and Jamieson, 1995; 1998) provides at least some reassurance of their validity. Students in my case study, especially boys and lower rather than higher ability pupils, believe that Academic Tutoring has been beneficial to their learning and communication skills. That said, it is more realistic to regard it as one of the 'carefully blended ingredients' than a 'magic bullet' that caused GCSE results to improve.

The considerable variations between tutor groups show that the preparation of teachers to play their part in Academic Tutoring must not be neglected. As the system becomes more embedded in a school, staff confidence and a reservoir of expertise will begin to build up. However the needs of tutors new to the school will still need to be met. There is therefore a strong case for including an introduction to Academic Tutoring in all Initial Teacher Education. However a note of caution must be sounded. Where Academic Tutoring has worked best it has developed at school level as an integrated part of school improvement. Any involvement of central government must support such efforts, allowing flexibility rather than imposing compulsion and regimentation.

Helena Romanes School, Essex Local Education Authority

Source: Fraser, 1999

Issues arising from the case study

What we find most striking in the case study is the evidence from young people that the success of individual tutoring depends on clear goals, focus, structure and time for them to talk.

Important outcomes are an increase in higher levels of achievement, raising confidence, more effective communication skills and for teachers an increase in the status of the tutors' role.

Unsuccessful experiences are characterized as 'a useless chat' or teacher dominated discussion. Tony Fraser underscores the positive correlation between tutor domination in interviews and pupils' lack of belief in the benefits of academic tutoring.

What was surprising was that the processes of tutoring were sometimes uncomfortable for students and therefore not very popular, but not disliked, and in response to suggestions for improvement requests for longer or more frequent interviews outnumbered all other suggestions (38 per cent girls, 28 per cent boys). The benefits of tutoring appeared more widespread for boys.

We now examine four features arising from this case study: preparation by the learner, finding time for tutorial conversations, support for the professional development of teachers and integrating the work with other aspects of the school.

Preparation by the learner

Tony Fraser's case study reveals that preparation by the learner is important. Preparation by young people can be carried out in group tutorial periods in the form group. Preparation includes discussing the rationale for individual tutoring, clarifying the goals, and examining the process. This will encourage the young people's commitment to individual tutoring and may help them feel more relaxed about talking about the learning. Preparation may be particularly important for Year 7 students. Val Dagley points out that these students were less confident in discussion, perhaps because they did not know their tutor very well:

> Well, as a first interview it was exciting and thoughts are going through your head, such as what is he going to ask me. Will it be good? Bad things, have I done any bad things? You worry sometimes about what to say and do. It's all right in the end but it does make you think about what the tutor is writing down. There's nothing to be scared about. (Boy, Year 7, Dagley, 2000)

This comment identifies a number of concerns that young people may experience. We note the fact that the tutor's record seems to be private and suggest that a record of the tutorial needs to be a joint and shared responsibility and its purpose explained, for example, 'Let's keep a record to remind ourselves what we said'.

In order to become more effective and make the best use of the time it is helpful if the learner can come to the tutorial prepared. This encourages the learner to take responsibility for the learning, be more active in the process, develop a sense of collaboration with the tutor (whether this is a teacher or peer) and be more skilled in meta-learning. As we discussed in Chapter 1, these four elements are those which characterize effective learning. The learner can help make the conversation more effective by going through the prompts (see Table 5.1) and making a few notes before the tutorial. In whole class preparation aspects of the learning conversation could be practised. This has two benefits:

- helping young people extend their use of the language of learning;
- developing confidence in learning conversations.

After individual tutoring has taken place it is useful to reflect with the whole tutor group on the value and usefulness of the process. To do this the discussion can return to the rationale and goals to see if the practice matches up and see if the rationale, goals or practice need to be refined before the next session. This needs to be seen as part of the learning cycle showing how the *Do, Review, Learn and Apply* cycle can be used to support learning.

Val Dagley (2000) found a difference between the focus at Key Stage 3 and Key Stage 4 during interviews. Key Stage 3 students reported more use of self-assessment forms as a basis for the interviews. As well as the common topics of lessons, homework, behaviour, targets and teachers, the interviews with students in Year 10 concentrated more on coursework, revision, GCSEs and careers. Evidence from Tony Fraser's case study suggests that some students already know how to review their work on their own, but we argue that talking enriches learning. Opportunities for young people to talk together about the learning that emerges from these discussions is important as together they can make links across their learning. In Chapter 7 we include a case study written by Barbara Patilla, a head of year, who talks about how her tutor team helps young people develop skills in reviewing learning – skills which she says need practising.

Further preparation can include opportunities for young people to practise together and indeed peer tutoring and peer group tutoring can supplement or replace learning conversations with the tutor.

Finding time for tutoring

Tony Fraser's case study reinforces the importance of the school's commitment to the scheme if it is to be successful. Finding time for tutoring within the school day is often problematic. This may mean abandoning some other aspect of school life.

Any model adopted will have advantages and disadvantages and schools will have to work out their own compromise between the ideal and the practical. Tutoring should be seen as teaching time as it requires professional preparation and proper attention to its process. It is a skilled task with important outcomes for learners (Betterton and Nash, 1996). In Table 5.3 we list the different ways schools find time for tutoring occasions.

Val Dagley notes that there are important structural and organizational issues arising for schools when trying to find time for individual tutoring.

> Practicalities of innovations are often very high on teachers' agendas. In this case many found that they were unable to keep up with the interview schedule set by the head teacher. Unless the tutor was very committed to arranging and conducting the interviews, it was very easy for other urgent matters to take up the assembly time (when the interviews were scheduled). Similarly considerable time and effort was needed to collect all the supporting materials for the interviews and to ensure recording and follow-up. One tutor said in his notes to me that 'while being a good idea in theory, it has been plagued by logistical nightmares'. (Dagley, 2000)

In Chapter 7 we return to the issue of pastoral heads finding time for tutoring. In the case study in that chapter we notice how even the most committed teachers, who view the time spent with individual young people as extremely valuable, find other aspects of school life erode the time allotted to tutoring.

Table 5.3 *Finding time for tutoring*

Model	Comments
Devoted day	Teachers meet with students throughout the day; students attend only for their programmed slot
Suspension of lessons	Attendance by students only for interview. All students and tutors focus on this at the same time. Preparation time can be done in as a group (e.g. PSHE lesson)
Withdrawal from lessons	One or two lessons per week of tutor time is allocated. Disruptive to students' timetable
Withdrawal from tutor time or PSHE	Requires cover or co-tutors. Can disrupt the tutorial or PSHE programme. May connect to group work in tutor or PSHE programme
Using assembly time	Tutors and students do not attend assemblies but use the time for learning conversations
Differential lunch hours	Tutors use part of the lunch break for individual tutorials
Early finish	One shorter day each week enables tutorials to take place
Early mornings	Before the start of the school day
End-on	At end of school day
Dedicated lesson	One lesson a week, all tutors work with students involved either in tutoring or cover classes
Group tutoring	This form can help develop the learning community
Peer tutoring	Develops skills and reciprocity in learners

Issues for teachers' professional development

In our discussions with teachers we have noted that some feel unprepared for the tutoring role. Other research supports this finding:

> Although some training in interview techniques had been provided for all staff, it was obvious that some were more confident and skilled than others. One tutor said, 'I have not found this easy. This is not a skill that I have'. It may be that some teachers are more comfortable with the large group, class teaching situation, for which they have been trained, than with one-to-one interviews. (Dagley, 2000)

In order for teachers to feel confident they may need time for professional development, preparation, support and time to discuss with colleagues issues that concern them. We have found that teachers respond enthusiastically in discussions about all the aspects we cover in this chapter.

Professional development opportunities can help overcome many of the problems and pitfalls associated with tutoring. Discussion in a supportive environment about these and other issues helps teachers decide appropriate strategies together for their particular school context and such conversations can decrease teachers' sense of isolation.

The following are common concerns:

- Tutors can be tempted to see tutorials as either 'therapy' or for 'nagging'.
- The process for the tutor and the learner may be uncomfortable.
- Learners may wish to choose a different tutor.
- Not knowing what to do when students raise difficulties they are having with other teachers.
- The tutor feels she or he must provide solutions.
- The tutor is uncomfortable with silences.
- It is hard to start the conversation.
- There is no clarity about goals for the session or about who decides on the agenda.
- Confidentiality.
- Getting caught up in the issue and not moving through the cycle.
- Frequency – one or even two tutorials a year is not enough.

We have found that teachers welcome opportunities to practise and develop tutoring skills, by working with peers, being observed and discussing feedback, by observing others, reviewing how they have worked, getting feedback from tutees, trying and reviewing different approaches. As tutors become more experienced they feel confident about departing from scripts and getting beyond the initial responses.

One innovative professional development occasion (Dagley, 2000) centred around the use of transcripts of tutoring conversations (see the example below).

Example   Professional development activity

The most useful source of data was when four members of staff and some students agreed to tape-record their interviews for me. This enabled me to hear what was actually said during the sessions, rather than what people remembered about them or chose to put on a questionnaire. However, I am aware that the discussions were undoubtedly influenced by the fact that all participants knew that I, as Deputy Head, was going to be listening to the tapes.

With prior permission from all concerned, sections of the anonymized interview transcripts were used for staff training role play. One teacher read through the tutor's words, one the student's and one was an observer. There were some tricky moments when some staff tried to identify tutors in the transcripts from the language used and the topics raised. In one case guesses were correct, in another not. However, in spite of this problem the exercise provoked a lot of discussion about the interviews, as well as being fun. The written feedback from the trios showed that there could be few more powerful ways of convincing teachers of how much many of them dominate and lead discussions with students.

The key points that emerged were used to produce a set of guidelines for the next student/tutor meeting.

Approach to the meeting:
 1 Let the students talk.
 2 Listen.
 3 Don't worry about periods of silence.
 4 Arrange the seating in a way that is conducive to conversation.
 5 Be aware of your body language.
 6 Be friendly, be warm, be sympathetic.
 7 Emphasize issues related to the students' learning.
 8 Don't gossip or discuss other students.
 9 Encourage students to suggest ways that they can improve.
 10 Emphasize the positive.
 11 Be honest and accurate.
 12 Be specific about future targets and strategies for the student.
 13 Try to defuse any problems or aggression.
 14 Suggest future meetings with you or other staff if necessary.
 15 Refer to senior staff in hall if necessary.
 16 Keep strictly to time, no more that 12 minutes each.

Source: Dagley, 2000

The most striking aspect of this example is the way in which the teachers became aware of the way in which they were dominating and leading discussions with students (transmission model) in the tutorial conversation. Talking through the transcript was a powerful way of identifying the trap that teachers can fall into in a tutorial. Transmission is the dominant model of teaching and talking may be so much part of the teachers' role that, as in this example, teachers may not be aware of how much time in a conversation they take up. Tutor domination was also an important finding in Tony Fraser's case study, which resulted in the pupils questioning the value of tutoring.

The set of guidelines the teachers drew up after analysing the transcripts demonstrate a shift to a constructivist model, for example, let the students talk; listen; do not worry about periods of silence; arrange the seating in a way that is conducive to conversation. This shift alters the pattern of teacher and student relationships. The teachers were also identifying ways in which students can be involved in making suggestions rather than this being the teacher's responsibility. This shared responsibility is fundamental in the changing balance of power amongst young people, teachers and parents (see Chapter 6).

Another aspect that Dagley identifies in her research is how the tutoring process is triggering issues about relationships between teachers and young people and the teachers' disciplinarian role (see example below).

Example   Extract from a tutorial conversation

It seemed that the variations in the nature and outcomes of some of the interviews were related to the different personalities of tutors and students and their relationships. One student wrote: 'My tutor doesn't like me and is always telling me off.' Unless skilfully handled the behaviour management role of the tutor can obviously mitigate against a productive academic interview. In one of the transcripts the following comment was made:

> Tutor: Honestly, I mean, you know what we think of these one-to-ones, I mean I may be calling you whatever out there but once we are in here I want you to work out what it is that makes you tick.
>
> This tutor was trying to separate the interview from her disciplinarian role and some of the rest of the tape, which includes quite a bit of shared laughter, suggests that she had some success.
>
> *Source*: Dagley, 2000

This and earlier examples highlight the need for reflection in tutor team meetings or professional development workshops on some of the pitfalls of tutoring practices. Opportunities for tutors to reflect on tutorials, learn together and adapt their practices can provide invaluable support. It is important that young people also have these opportunities for review and a chance to give feedback to their tutors.

Integrating tutoring with other aspects of school life

As Tony Fraser's and Val Dagley's research suggests, the process of tutoring will be more successful when other aspects of the school support the development of discussion about learning. There are issues about structure, monitoring and evaluation that are significant.

Important links can be made with other systems and processes in school, for example, group tutoring, IEPs, learning and teaching policies, subject teaching, the culture of lessons and meetings with parents which focus on learning. Personal-social education can provide a forum for discussions about learning and may be used to help young people prepare for tutoring.

Using her research data Dagley generated a sheet of issues to encourage reflection and to generate ideas among staff and young people (see Table 5.4).

Table 5.4   *Issues for staff discussion*

- Are we clear about the purpose of these interviews? Are they to build relationships, monitor behaviour, to solve problems or to set targets?
- What might be the most appropriate arrangements, for example, interviews on a one-to-one basis, in pairs or in small groups?
- In what ways might student planners be used?
- How might a learning record be kept of the interview?
- How could we collect evidence of improved performance and any possible links with the interviews?
- How might we find out if any of the skills are being transferred to other areas of school life – by staff or by students?
- In what ways are the interviews changing over time, as relationships build?
- What might be the connection between these interviews and the new parents' evenings?

Tony Fraser's and Val Dagley's research are examples of the way in which some schools are monitoring and evaluating the effectiveness of tutoring occasions. Other schools could carry out similar ways of monitoring, perhaps not in so much depth, or build in a time for review, as we suggest in our 'Preparation by the learner' section. Time is a scarce resource and schools need to check out if individual tutoring time is well spent and how it is enhancing young people's learning.

Closing thoughts

Individual tutoring cannot fix a culture that does not encourage learning or learning conversations across all activities (Gray et al., 1999). In Chapter 9 we discuss the idea of learning communities and emphasize the school's need to develop talk about learning; young people and their teachers need to become fluent in a learning language. Some schools are more successful in supporting learning within Personal Learning Planning (Bullock and Wikeley, 2000). These schools tend to recognize and explicitly acknowledge individual tutoring as an initiative for learning. The students here have begun to understand the wider implications of such activities.

In such a community, tutoring is integrated into the school. It is not an add-on. In a learning community, all members are involved in learning conversations, for example, teachers taking part in developmental appraisal processes. Teachers involved in learning conversations with each other develop skills that enable them to facilitate learning with young people.

Recent research into the most improving schools (Gray et al., 1999) suggests that these schools are developing systematic and long-term investigations and experiments into teaching and learning. The research carried out by Val Dagley and Tony Fraser demonstrates different ways in which schools are investigating their systems of individual tutorials and are helping students learn more effectively as a result.

Notes

1 This chapter is an extended version of a broadsheet: Carnell and Lodge (2000). The broadsheet forms the basis of the chapter and is developed to connect with many themes contained in the book. We would like to thank all the teachers who took part in the NAPCE Academic Tutoring and Becoming a Form Tutor workshops. Their contributions on the courses helped develop the broadsheet and chapter.

Further reading

Rudduck, J., Chaplain, R. and Wallace, G. (1996) *School Improvement: What Can Pupils Tell Us?* London: David Fulton.
Watkins, C., Carnell, E., Lodge, C., Wagner, P. and Whalley, C. (2000) *Learning about Learning: Resources for Supporting Effective Learning*. London: Routledge Falmer.

6
Connecting Learning

Connecting learning is about helping young people identify and make sense of their experiences across a number of different contexts. The advantages of connecting learning is that learners can extend their thinking, enrich their understanding in a more holistic way, develop more insights about themselves as learners and come to a better understanding of their own learning. Connecting learning is an important aspect of effective learning and schools have a pivotal role.

As Bentley points out, schools, along with all those involved in education, need to develop more complex understandings about learning: 'We are moving from the view that learning takes place only inside people's heads, or inside single institutions designed for the purpose. The reality is much more complex and unpredictable – initially more threatening and riskier, but also potentially far richer and more rewarding' (Bentley, 1998: 157).

In examining the concept of 'connecting learning' we consider three interrelated themes: the differences in learning in different contexts; connecting learning across different contexts; and extending this connecting process to the systematic involvement of others, especially parents, who support young people's learning outside school. We examine the challenges that connecting learning poses for schools. In doing so we try and make sense of three anomalies:

- Different contexts invite differences in learning. Young people engage in learning activities in very different ways when they are learning outside school compared with learning in school. Their learning may be more effective outside school, yet, academic school learning is often perceived by teachers and young people as superior.
- In school young people are rarely asked to articulate any connection between their school learning and the rest of their lives, yet learning in school is influenced and enhanced by the wider social context. Young people may not fully appreciate the influences that different contexts have on each other.

- Parents are young people's first teachers yet there are few effective structures in secondary schools to draw on parents' expertise as teachers and to encourage collaboration between teachers and parents to enhance young people's learning.

While schools can make a difference to young people's learning, what happens outside schools is most significant in determining school success and in influencing life chances (MacBeath, 2000). To disregard young people's learning outside school is to lose valuable opportunities to enrich learning and help develop connected and holistic learning experiences.

The differences in learning in different contexts

In Chapter 2 we consider some differences between learning inside and outside school, suggesting that in-school learning is more cognitively oriented, highly paced, directed and controlled by the teacher, incremental and cumulative, rigidly defined and highly boundaried. In contrast, learning outside school is less boundaried and includes practical and emotionally-charged elements. For example, think of the boy ballet dancer *Billy Elliot* in the film of the same name. Later in the chapter we refer to other research that examines the difference between school learning and home learning in the section on young people learning with parents in the home.

Out of school the learner often has much more control – over pace, direction, definition, content and so forth. We argue that school learning needs to be more like this as these characteristics are more likely to be effective; they invite learners to be active, responsible and collaborative. These characteristics match the constructivist and co-constructivist models of learning. The learners' experiences are more connected as learners construct meaning and understanding from their wider experiences. The reception model does not invite collaborative learning or connections across the learners' experiences and contexts.

Learning outside school

Schools need to recognize the complexity and unpredictability of young people's learning experiences, to use Bentley's words, by talking with young people about what they are learning out of school. Teachers do not often examine the rich learning experiences young people have outside school, for example:

- social development: relationships, trust, separations, conflict, group and team learning;
- personal responsibility: being responsible for themselves and others, living in the community;
- employment: managing their finances;
- life transitions: a birth or death in the family, changing schools;

- political understanding: understanding the role of society;
- acquiring expertise: computers, sports, using their expertise to teach others;
- developing expressive skills: music, dancing, drama.

Analysing this list of just a small sample of the things young people learn outside school indicates how emotionally, practically and socially oriented their learning is. Learnings of these sorts take place slowly over time, are unpredictable, complex and cross many different boundaries. These sorts of learnings take place in situations such as youth clubs, sports teams, choir, community activities as well as very informal situations such as with the family, friends and other social and local groups. They also learn on their own, for example when carrying out Internet searches or reading.

The media offers great potential for learning outside school. Young people may spend more time watching television than they do in other out-of-school activities, for example, talking with their parents, siblings or friends. Over 66 per cent of teenagers use the Internet at home (Cassidy, 2001). The Internet opens up new ways in which young people can talk to others around the world and carry out research on a massive scale. While we often hear of the risks the Internet may pose, we do not often hear how such technology can be a major source of learning for young people.

The school may not recognize or ever see the expertise and understandings that young people have, and may underestimate young people's learning outside school or the responsibility they have. Schools need to appreciate the whole picture of each young person and to value the learning they accomplish outside school.

One of us learned a very important lesson as a naive, newly qualified teacher. Some concern arose about a pupil in Year 7 who, although engaged in his learning and extremely cheerful, was sometimes late to school, dressed in clothes that were rather shabby and who seemed undernourished. She decided to talk to his parents at the first parents' meeting. When this boy's parents did not show up she made an appointment to visit them at home. She discovered the boy lived with his grandparents; neither parent was around. His grandfather was blind and his grandmother was a wheelchair user. This 11-year-old boy cared for them both, ran the household, did the shopping and cleaning. He got himself to school after making breakfast for them all and after doing his homework at night prepared the family dinner. School was just a small part of his very busy and responsible world. It was learned that it was important to focus on his learning rather than see him as a problem.

This example highlights the importance of schools needing to understand the history, social, environmental, economic, demographic and political life of the school's community and its importance in the lives of young people. As Rudduck and her colleagues point out, the context of school can often be discordant with other, highly significant aspects of young people's lives:

> What pupils have told us in interview is that while teachers are for the most part supportive, stimulating and selfless in the hours they put in to help young people,

the conditions of learning that are common across secondary schools do not adequately take account of the pressures they feel as they struggle to reconcile the demands of their social and personal lives with their development of their identity as learners. (Rudduck et al., 1996: 1)

To take account of the demands of young people's lives and the tensions these might produce in their development as learners the school needs to go beyond understanding. Schools need to value and enhance the contribution that their experiences out of school can make to their learning and to their overall development as young people.

We know that to ignore the social and emotional worlds of young people is to create a block to learning (see Chapter 3). Schools need to have in place structures, procedures and processes for gaining relevant information. But it is important to recognize, honour and respect young people's privacy and the self-consciousness of many young people, and this will change over their time in secondary school. Teachers need to use fine judgements and sensitivity about how they approach the youngsters.

How the context of learning affects young people's roles

Sometimes learning and teaching roles are reversed when young people are engaged in activities outside school, as many parents and teachers will recognize who have learned about computer and other technology from their children. We draw on an example to demonstrate how young people can take on leadership or teaching roles when learning occurs outside school and where a different relationship can develop between the young people and adults (see example below).

Example   Reversed roles in learning

Three lads came to see me wanting to start a guitar club. They wanted space to do it and support. They wanted to advertise it and run it themselves and a teacher to supervise. It was a spur of the moment thing but I suppose I intuitively recognized the opportunity it offered me. I volunteered to be the supervising teacher because I play the guitar myself. Badly I have to say. As the supervising teacher I had nothing to do except keep an eye on things, watch and listen. I became a regular member. They were a million miles ahead of me in guitar technique. They recognized that pretty quickly too and helped me along from where I was, not from their pinnacle of expertise. Gently but challengingly too. They were excellent teachers. They taught me so much. I think I learned a bit too about organization and teamwork and something about pedagogy as well.

Source: MacBeath and Myers, 1999, cited in MacBeath, 2000: 142

This example demonstrates the importance of recognizing the potential for young people to use their expertise in a way that probably does not often happen in the classroom. As MacBeath points out, this example tells us something important about learning and teaching and the relationship between teachers and learners:

> Its character here is closer to tutoring or coaching than to teaching. In this relationship there is a greater fluidity and interchangeability of teacher and learner roles. It is a microcosm of what a school might be like if it could exceed its conventional parameters and open up itself to the possibilities of collaborative learning. (MacBeath, 2000: 142)

This is a good example of a small community of learners where teachers and learners are supporting learning regardless of status, role position and accepted hierarchy. In other words it is more like a co-constructivist approach and more like learning out of school. The teacher in the above example is not threatened by the lads being 'a million miles ahead' but recognizes the potential for learning and the young people's ability to be teachers. In the classroom the learners' potential for teaching may not be tapped.

Connecting learning across different contexts

We argue that for most impact all learning experiences need to be valued and connected. In Chapter 4 we examine the role of the tutor in helping young people connect their learning across different subjects to make learning more coherent in school. Here we go further by suggesting that learning in school needs to connect with learning outside school. As Resnick puts it:

> there is growing evidence, then, that not only may schooling not contribute in a direct and obvious way to performance outside school, but also that knowledge acquired outside school is not always used to support in-school learning. School is coming to look increasingly isolated from the rest of what we do. (Resnick, 1987: 15)

In this section we focus on how the school can help young people make connections between their learning experiences within and outside school. This will result in learning being more effective for young people as it will be more coherent and holistic.

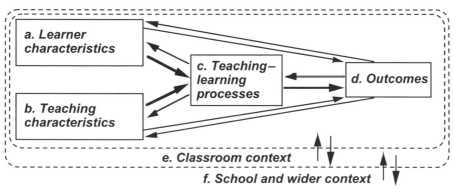

Figure 6.1   *A contextual model for school learning (Watkins et al., 1996) developed from Biggs and Moore, 1993)*

We find it useful to consider a contextual model of school learning (Figure 6.1) because it reminds us that learners, the teaching–learning processes and learning outcomes are all interconnected and influenced by their context. While the model has two-way arrows across the wider context, connections between in school and out of school learning may not often be made. Year 7 students talking about their learning outside school during a research project seemed surprised to be asked how it connected with their school experiences. They appeared to see learning outside school as a very separate experience from learning inside (Lodge, 1997).

As Bentley (1998) suggests, teachers (and young people) must embrace the implications of the idea that learning does not takes place only inside single institutions designed for that purpose. This can be challenging for schools, as he indicates. But when learning outside is connected with learning inside school it can be hugely valuable as teachers have witnessed helping young people learn from work experience, or through high-quality PSHE. Examples of these include young people's personal-social experiences connecting with such themes as relationships, conflict, group dynamics and so forth.

Young people's learning outside school can be enhanced by using the *Do, Review, Learn and Apply* cycle we discuss throughout this book. When returning from their work experience teachers can help young people reflect, identify the learning and think about how they might apply that learning to future situations. There may also be benefits from the emphasis on participation in school and community-based activities required by the inclusion of Citizenship in the National Curriculum from 2002. The opportunities that these provide extend young people's learning in important ways through working in different settings in the school and outside community. But learning may not happen at the time of the activity. If these community-based activities, like work experience, are to be effective for young people they need to be reviewed explicitly as learning opportunities and not seen as ends in themselves. The role the school can play in helping young people understand these sorts of learning experiences is highly valuable.

Connecting vertical and horizontal dimensions

MacBeath points out that the continued inability of schools to make a significant difference for young people may be explained by their 'vertical' and 'horizontal' dimensions: 'The 'horizontal' relationship is in the connections between school and community and is tested by the permeability of the boundaries between home and classroom, school and street. The 'vertical' relationship is what ties schools into an upward progression, nursery to primary, primary to secondary, secondary to college and university' (MacBeath, 2000: 139–40).

We argue that to enhance young people's learning the horizontal and vertical relationships need to be addressed explicitly. Effective learners know how to take the learning from one situation and apply it to another. This transfer of learning does not happen automatically and schools can help young people learn how to make connections happen (see Chapter 4). As Gardner points out, a successful student: 'knows how to use opportunities for learning which are distributed throughout his or her environment. This includes not only books and libraries, media and electronic information but the learning resources of people – teachers, friends, family, mentors and employers' (Gardner, 1983: 35).

In *Learning about Learning* (Watkins et al., 2000) we describe a number of activities which can help young people develop connections between learning here and now and their lives outside and after school. This is a way of addressing the 'vertical' and 'horizontal' dimensions that MacBeath identifies. We suggest that young people review together the similarities and differences between learning in these two dimensions and contexts, especially under the headings:

- purposes;
- strategies used;
- effects;
- feelings;
- contexts.

Learners are invited to consider the differences between learning in and out of school (the horizontal dimension). They are asked to identify the things that support learning in school (such as specialist facilities, equipment and teachers; structured learning programmes and learning in groups). They are asked to identify the things that support out of school learning (such as more choice of time, place and who one associates with for the learning, more flexibility in time, pace and changing tack, more control over time). Finally they are invited to consider what they can learn from one context to apply to another, and to identify new learning strategies appropriate to each.

A time-line activity (see Watkins et al., 2000) is designed to help young people think about learning as a lifelong process (the vertical dimension). The young people interview older people about their experiences of learning after leaving school. The responses are then considered, and young people are invited to identify what they have discovered from them, including connecting with their own experiences. Finally they are asked to consider their own ideas about learning after they have left school. (The phrase *long-life* learning was found by one of us in a student's examination paper. We like the way it jolts and then adds to our thinking about learning throughout people's lives.)

Other strategies teachers have developed to promote connections and coherence are reflective journals and learning logs (see Chapter 1) to help the young people build a meta-learning account of their learning in different contexts. The teacher can support this by monitoring and reviewing with the young person. There are many occasions when teachers can invite written or spoken review of connections in their learning (see Chapter 5).

Work experience, activity programmes, school journeys, community programmes and so on are other strategies that involve young people learning in other contexts. We argue these kinds of experiences are only the start of opening up learning to a much wider set of experiences. What is important is how these experiences are reviewed and understood.

Connecting learning to young people's everyday lives

We have already remarked that it is not common for young people to make connections between different learning contexts. Young people say they like learning when it connects to their lives. However, this is often not made explicit by teachers so they struggle to make the connections. Consider the following example, which is an extract from an interview with some Year 10 students. Earlier in the interview we had discussed a lesson on *Othello*.

Example   Connecting learning to young people's everyday lives

Q: When does it feel good to be learning?
Boy 1: I did a first aid course last weekend and you feel oh yeah I can use this now if I see someone there on the floor. And you feel happy with yourself because you know you have learned something that you can use. Personally this stuff about Iago once we've finished the subject I'm never going to use it again in my life.
Boy 2: I think that about maths lessons as well. Algebra and stuff! You don't learn about how to do a tax return or something. A tax return, I'm going to use that. Algebra: x minus two x times three. When are you going to use that?
Girl: I mean I think of a situation, if you are talking to your secretary you're not exactly going to say [changes to posh stagy voice] Oh Iago thought that . . .
(Lodge, 2001).

It is interesting that in response to the first question, *When does it feel good to be learning?*, they all stated that it feels good when learning is connected.

Despite their reservation about studying *Othello*, the students report that they enjoyed the lesson. They had been making connections between how men talk about women in the past and in the present. Nevertheless, the purposes of studying this play were not clear to them, nor the purposes of studying algebra, in contrast to taking the first aid course. It is clear from this short extract that the young people found it difficult to make connections between learning in school and their lives without being clear about the purposes of their learning.

Young people can and will make connections between what they learn in school and their own lives. But if they are not able to then the teacher needs to be specific about the connections. Not all learning can be connected with their lives. In such cases the purposes for learning needs to be clear. Young people have faith that what schools give them to learn has relevance; there is a rationale. This is in line with the reception model of learning where young people rely on the teacher to tell them what they need to know. Whereas in the constructivist and co-constructivist models young people need to make sense and develop meaning for themselves with help from the teacher. In other chapters (see specifically Chapters 1 and 2) we cite research that indicates that young people engage most effectively when learning connects with their lives.

Teachers and parents as partners in supporting young people's learning

The idea of parents and teachers as partners in supporting young people's learning may not sit comfortably with some teachers. Throughout the history of education we can trace a very strong boundary division between teachers and parents. Take for example the following explanation:

> One of the main themes of the mental hygiene literature of the 1920s is parent blaming. Hygienists made a direct causal connection between parents' treatment of children and all subsequent psychological or behavioural disorders. The seeds of maladjustment were sown in childhood. No child escaped the home unscarred. The faults of parents were many. Regardless of good intentions, parents did harm. (Cohen, 1989: 18)

While this view may sound extreme today, the boundary division is still strong in some people's perceptions as the following extract indicates. Here Alan Bennett paints a picture of parent–teacher relationships when describing a 'Meet the Parents' week:

> That was the real point of these get-togethers. The teachers were appalled by the parents but found their shortcomings reassuring. With parents like these, they reasoned, who could blame the schools? The parents, recalling their own teachers as figures of dignity and authority, found the staff sloppy. Awe never entered into it, apparently. 'Too human by half' was their verdict. So both Nature and Nurture came away, if not satisfied, at any rate absolved. 'Do you wonder?' said the teachers, looking at the parents. 'They get it at school,' said the parents. (Bennett, 2000: 11–12)

It is as if teachers and parents inhabit completely different worlds. Here we see two sides apportioning blame and responsibility to the other. Parents and teachers are seen as having many faults. The teachers see the parents as doing harm. The parents think teachers have lost their authority. There is no sense of meeting in the interests of the young people's learning or to help them connect their learning experiences.

Parents sense this negative view especially when things go wrong for their children: 'Parents are viewed negatively as a hazard to children's education. I think if the child is doing well this is not a problem, but as soon as there is a problem of any kind it is' (parent of 16-year-old boy, quoted in Askew, 2000: 115). The main problem identified by Askew is that the goal of most communications from school to home is not clear to the parents, nor is it clear how parents can make use of communications to support their child's learning. The dominant model of communication between school and parents emerging from her research is 'correction'. When correction is the primary motive for communication, it is likely that the underlying approach to learning in the school is the reception model (see Chapter 1). In this model teachers are the experts. Parents are viewed as passive recipients of information. There is an imbalance of power between teacher and parent: 'Power is both implicit and explicit in relationships between parents and professional educators even in situations where both parties have a common goal in supporting the education of a child' (Todd and Higgins, 1998: 235).

The power of the expert may have worked for both teacher and parent in the past, but Todd and Higgins suggest professionals now need the opportunity to have a less fixed view of themselves and their role to allow a flexible mutuality between parents and teachers. This flexible mutuality may seem to teachers to be chaotic and risky as it involves the school letting go of some of its power and recognizing the parents' contribution to their children's learning and to the teachers' learning (Askew, 2000).

In order to shift the focus from seeing parents as people who either get young people prepared to learn in school, or who fix miscreants, or are even obstacles to learning we draw on the ideas of Wolfendale. Her approach signifies an important shift in appreciating and valuing the parents' pivotal role in children's learning (see Table 6.1).

Table 6.1 *Reasons why parents should be more involved in school*

- Parents are the primary educators of their children and are experts on their children.
- Parents often have vital information and insights concerning their children.
- Parents want to co-operate.
- Parent and teacher skills complement one another.
- Involvement of parents should include decision-making, not simply information giving.
- Parents want to do what they believe to be in their child's best interests.
- Parents will respond to invitations to participate in school if they can see the benefit to their child.
- All parents have a right to be involved and to contribute.
- All parents care about their children's welfare and well-being. The tiny minority who appear not to care do so either because of stress in their lives or because their own experience of schooling was negative and left them with fears and anxieties about school.

Source: Wolfendale, 1992.

It is important to be reminded of the fact that parents are the primary educators and experts on their children. We have much to learn from them. Salmon (1998) points out that Vygotsky's vision of school learning which calls on children's potential, rather than their actual level of accomplishment, is inspired by exactly the same principles that intuitively guide parents in their interactions with very young children:

Just as mothers attribute to their infants capacities that they do not as yet possess, so teachers, in Vygotsky's portrayal, need to treat their pupils as far more competent than they presently are. And just as babies come to acquire the powers of understanding their mothers already see in them, so school learners will grow into the competences with which their teachers credit them. (Salmon, 1998: 102)

Unlike the generous attributions of parents, Salmon suggests, schooling typically underestimates its learners: 'school learning typically treats learners as less able than they feel themselves to be' (Salmon, 1998: 101).

Consultation and collaborative models of working with parents

Echoing the stance taken by Salmon and Wolfendale in recognizing the parents' expertise in their children's learning, Askew (2000) suggests that schools need to adopt different communication models with parents. As important alternatives to the 'correction' model, the 'consultation' and 'collaborative' models identify a shift in the balance of power between teachers and parents. The involvement of parents in these models includes decision-making, not simply information giving.

In the 'consultation' model there is some commitment to developing a partnership with parents and recognition that this is important for young people's learning. (The same term is used in Chapter 3 by Patsy Wagner, the educational psychologist, when she describes her work with schools.) In this model there is a stress on making connections and developing meaning (the constructivist approach to learning, see Chapter 1). This model recognizes the fact that parents have vital information and insights concerning their children (Wolfendale, 1992) and draws on parents' knowledge about their children.

The collaborative model takes the partnership with parents a stage further. Here it is recognized that learning outside of school is equally important as learning in school. In a collaborative relationship teachers' and parents' skills are seen to complement each other (Wolfendale, 1992) and teachers and parents are seen as learning together. Each is an expert on their own learning and has a valid perspective and understanding of young people. They can give useful feedback to each other (Askew, 2000).

Collaborative relationships are based on co-constructivist approaches to learning (see Chapter 1). This suggests the idea of learning conversations in which all the participants are learners. Co-construction implies a two-way exchange and involves a shift in perception of young people, teachers and parents and their roles (Askew, 2000).

Parents' knowledge in supporting teachers

Parents know their children in different situations, and this knowledge can be helpful to the school. Parents have knowledge about the children in greater depth and breadth than teachers, knowledge about their emotional, physical and spiritual dispositions. They have knowledge of the home situation that has an impact on young people's learning in school. Teachers can support the young people better when they have parts of this knowledge.

This connecting process can be strengthened by inviting parents to be partners with the schools in supporting young people's learning. Even the bureaucratic models such as home–school agreements can help this process if discussion between parents and teachers arises from them (Budge, 2000).

Young people learning with parents in the home

Learning outside school most often matches the co-constructivist model. This is because learning at home, for example, is less formal and there is not such a rigid view about the roles of 'teacher' and 'learner'. Learning is integrated into family life. The physical arrangements help the family communicate easily. People may be more relaxed both mentally and physically compared with in the classroom. The nature of the talk is informal. It is organic in nature, free-flowing and there is no sense of a right answer; everyone's views are valid.

The following examples provide an insight into the ways in which learning conversations happen around the kitchen table in marked contrast to the classroom.

Examples   Learning in the home

We had to think of a plot by ourselves and I couldn't think of anything and my Mum and my Mum's boyfriend and a neighbour all sat in the kitchen and they all started arguing and that helps me learn. Like it is one to one, no really it's more than that. In the classroom it is with one teacher with a load of students but at home it is like so many teachers and just me as part of it. I think it is much better. In the classroom you can just fade away into the background. You can sit there and do a bit of work or not. But if you are in a situation with your family you can't possible sit there and not be part of what's going on. There were a lot more ideas than you would get in class.

Q: Does this sort of conversation happen in lessons?

No way. You are expected to behave differently in class. You have to sit up straight and wait for your turn with the teacher.

 With a teacher they have got an aim of what they want you to come up with. But if you are talking just generally about one thing that leads on to talking about another thing, then something completely different. My Granddad walked in and then he said something else that no one had thought of and it just took off. I was learning so much from all the different points of view. (Year 10 female)

Another young person makes a similar point:

My Dad's best friend really helped me. I worked with him for a long time. Even though the teachers are really good they sort of just put it in your head. They do explain it to you, but when you know the person better and when you are outside school and you don't sort of have to be sitting up straight and listening,

---

> you are able to relax. They casually explain it to you and you can talk back and compare it with what you think and it is much more helpful. (Year 10 female)
>
> *Source*: Carnell, 2000

In these situations we can see that the learning relationships and physical environments are different from those at school. Moving across the physical boundaries of the school may represent a very real difference for some young people in the way in which they learn. School may be a place where young people feel uncomfortable or anxious and their emotions may get in the way of learning. As we see in Sally Wells's example in Chapter 3 the school itself may inhibit young people's learning by the way it is structured and the particular behaviours school imposes on students. There may be a variety of reasons why young people's learning in school may be disconnected. The physical conditions will affect young people's learning either positively or negatively.

Earlier we discussed the difference between learning in and out of school. We now draw on research that compares school and home as contexts for learning to illustrate some other important differences (see Table 6.2).

Table 6.2   *School and home as contexts for learning*

School learning	Home learning
• Shaped by curriculum	• Shaped by interest
• Bounded by sanctions	• Spontaneous
• Timetabled	• Flexible
• Contrived problems	• Natural problems
• Restricted language	• Everyday language
• Limited conversations	• Extended conversations
• Special resources – limited access	• Natural resources – unlimited access
• Recognition of achievement in approved areas	• Recognition of achievement in many areas
• Horizontal age group	• Vertical age group
• Distant relationship with adults	• Close relationship with adults
• Pupil role	• Multiple roles
• Accounts for little variation in academic achievement	• Accounts for much variation in academic achievement

Source: Hannon, 1993, cited in Macbeath 2000: 141

As Salmon points out, the difference is not just a matter of the far more intimate personal relations that obtain at home:

> Beyond this, learning at home entails the sense of shared concerns, of joint endeavour. In teaching their children, parents (and other members of the family and friends) address them as if they were essentially like themselves; as sharing the same kind of subjectivity. This means seeing even the youngest children in terms of potentiality, rather than limitation. (Salmon, 1998: 99)

This indicates a great contrast to the notion held by teachers that ability is fixed. This challenges more than power structures but beliefs.

If learning conversations are adopted between parents, teachers and young people based around learning potential rather than limitation, then the benefits for all participants will be greater. In addition, many of the features of the out-of-school learning match the kind of dispositions which young people need to embrace to become effective learners.

Parents supporting school learning

Parents and others make a large contribution to supporting school learning. We know of situations where parents have been explicit in supporting their son's or daughter's learning. This may be in relation to the learning that young people are expected to do after school. It is interesting that this is often described as homework. One teacher we know has banned the word 'work' in the classroom and parents have been amused by their children asking them to help them with their home learning. Parents often help their children with research and other investigations and spend time gardening, fishing, doing car repairs, cooking and visiting museums and art galleries in order to be involved in and to support their children's learning.

Parents have also shown an interest in helping young people learn about their learning. For example, after attending a workshop on academic tutoring (see Chapter 5), one teacher said that he would use the learning conversation framework to help his daughter review her learning. Many parents look for such ways to support their children, and schools can support them becoming mentors in this way.

As we stress throughout this chapter, parents are the child's first teachers and they continue to help children learn throughout their lives. Parents have a potentially huge contribution to make to the child's learning in secondary school providing this is recognized explicitly by teachers and parents.

In the case study that follows, we present the example of a school that had made a determined effort to make connections with children's families. Although the case is from the primary phase, we believe that the school is involved in important activities which secondary schools could adapt.

This school has deliberately set out to help young people learn by connecting with their parents' enthusiasm and willingness to provide more support at home and in school. They also capitalize on parents' knowledge and experience of their young children to develop materials to help other parents support their children's learning. In this school, the partnership with parents went further than consultation to include collaboration on projects to improve the young people's learning. This readiness to see parents as part of a

---

Case study   Kings Norton Primary School

One of us was involved in research in a primary school in Birmingham that had made parental involvement a key process in their improvement plans. Parental involvement in this school was very high. Some of this was practical involvement in physical improvements, in courses run by the school and in an active PTA. Parents accompanied children on educational trips and visits and volunteered to help in classrooms. Many had jobs in the school. One parent commented that she probably spent more time in the school than in her home. The headteacher, Lorna Field, took the view that it was important to develop the skills of the parents because 'it has a knock-on effect with the children'.

Information provided for them was highly appreciated by the parents; from the introductory booklet provided before the children started, the information about their children's curriculum for the forthcoming year to progress reports. Attendance at the parents' evenings was very high – as much as 98 per cent.

The school also offered an extensive programme of courses for parents. This is part of a wider programme of involving parents in school. Some are typical of adult education provision such as computer and first aid courses, but others more directly related to parenting and schooling. A ten-week course on 'Your Child at School and You', and a 30-week course called 'Access to Classroom Assistants' had been attended by some of the parents interviewed. Participants on this course had revised some of the information pack given to parents when their child was preparing to come to the school. One parent intended to train as a teacher following attendance at a course offered by the school. A pattern appeared to be that parents would become involved in some aspect of the school, perhaps volunteer for some activity, then join a course, take up a paid job and then extend their skills through training.

Kings Norton Primary School, Birmingham Local Education Authority

---

learning community contributed to a very vibrant learning atmosphere in the school (see Chapter 9 where we discuss learning communities).

Closing thoughts

Three levels emerge in ways learning can be connected:

- Level 1: connecting learning in the classroom – making connections between what is learned in school and outside.
- Level 2: connecting learning with out of school activities – taking learners out of school to make connections. Young people visit other significant places where learning happens, for example, work experience or museum visits which form part of the school's learning programme. The learning is then connected with the learning in the classroom.
- Level 3: connecting learning as a continual process – this learning is connected across young people's lives and they are helped make sense of their learning in a more holistic way. The school boundary is less distinct as

learners move across, in and out of school as the goals, purposes and activities demand.

This third level of connection presents more difficulties for schools. It suggests a co-constructivist approach that depends on different sorts of non-hierarchical relationships and flatter school structures. To develop strategies to connect these experiences the school needs to consider the arrangement of times, relationships with adults, including the teacher, and the assessment and record-keeping processes.

In his book, *Learning Beyond the Classroom*, Bentley quotes an 18-year-old from Birmingham: 'The things you learn in school are to do with education and to get jobs. You are not really using them in actual real life' (Bentley, 1998: 1). He argues not just that the content of learning should be more useful for young people, but that the ways in which they learn should be more fitting for their futures. We agree with Bentley that if learning in schools is to make a contribution to the lives of young people, then organizational patterns and learning approaches must be challenged in order that young people's learning is more easily connected. In Chapters 7, 8 and 9 we examine what the school can do in organizational terms.

Further reading

Askew, S. (2000) 'Communications between school and home – correction, consultation or conversation for learning?', in S. Askew (ed.), *Feedback for Learning*. London: Routledge Falmer.

Bentley, T. (1998) *Learning Beyond the Classroom: Education for a Changing World*. London: Routledge.

Claxton, G. (1999) *Wise Up*. London: Bloomsbury.

7

Pastoral Teams and Learning

This chapter focuses on the role of pastoral teams and pastoral team leaders in supporting young people's learning. The potential contribution of the pastoral team has been neglected in schools and in writing about learning and about pastoral care. Here we explore the specific contribution of the pastoral team to the learning of young people.

We provide a rationale for this approach, together with examples from practice and our own research to illustrate the special role of the pastoral team. We include a case study in which a head of year reflects on how she and her team promote the learning of young people. We have omitted aspects of the pastoral team's work that is not directly related to learning, such as casework and administrative responsibilities. We have considered the personal-social curriculum only as far as it directly relates to learning about learning.

Although we focus on one aspect of the work of the team, we believe it must be integrated into the general pattern of teachers' work and into the life of the whole school. The connection at the whole-school level is important as Harrison (1998:23) suggests that improvement in pastoral care requires breaking down the barriers 'between pastoral care and academic frameworks within the school; between those who teach and those who learn; and between the school, its parents and its wider community'. This chapter considers some of the ways in which schools can consider integrating support for young people.

We look at these issues under the following headings:

- the context for pastoral teams;
- working in teams;
- the pastoral team;
- linking the team with the rest of the school;
- developing the pastoral team;
- the pastoral leader.

The context for pastoral teams

Since the 1988 Education Reform Act (ERA) the emphasis has been on the development of the curriculum, on teaching and on students' performance. This led many of us working in the pastoral field to fear that pastoral teams would be disbanded and the role of tutor and pastoral team leader would be devalued or dispensed with. Indeed, the structures *were* disbanded in some schools. However, recent research by Best shows that pastoral structures are still commonly in place and still valued in the majority of secondary schools, although some of the associated titles may have changed (Best, 1999). We must remember that while titles change, roles do not always match the changes (Lodge, 1995). There is evidence, too, that the relative status of the head of year, as measured by the number of remuneration points on the pay scale, has been reduced in some schools.

Calvert and Henderson (1998) argue strongly that pastoral teams need to be managed, rather than merely maintained, while recognizing the resource restrictions within which team leaders have to manage. These can include:

- lack of time;
- lack of financial resources;
- little choice of team members;
- little commitment from team members;
- lack of support from senior or other colleagues.

Calvert (1998) argues that pastoral management and change are more complex than other management tasks in secondary schools because the work is less clearly defined, less tangible and has lower status than curriculum work. There has been an increasing emphasis in school improvement writing on the value of collaboration and of teamwork and generally on the importance of managing teams. Little of this, however, has been directly applied to managing pastoral teams.

Policy-makers have hardly considered the value of pastoral teams either,[1] but we can conclude from Best's research (1999) that they serve an essential function in schools or they would have disappeared. It is the development of the purposes and potential of the pastoral team to support young people's learning that we consider here.

Working in teams

This section looks at the value of teams in supporting young people's learning. We begin by asking the question: what is the pastoral team for? There are two parts to the answer. The first focuses on the value of teamwork and the second relates to the specific activities of the pastoral team. We will consider them in turn before making connections between them.

We do not intend here to repeat in detail what has been rehearsed about the value of teams in many management books (see for example Bell, 1992). But it is worth reminding ourselves of the main reasons why so many management gurus are enthusiastic about teams.

Teams have the potential to be more democratic. Members can share the workload. Teams can take ideas, projects and problem-solving further than a single person can. Team members have a structure within which they can support each other. They can provide a forum for professional development and for two-way communication between the manager and team members (Gold and Evans, 1998). Teams can support and help less experienced members by providing understanding, training, team teaching and professional development, and, if necessary, taking required disciplinary action. A good team leader will find ways of ensuring that membership of a team brings such advantages.

Unfortunately, teams do not always provide these advantages for their members. Pastoral teams come together as ad hoc arrangements of people whose main responsibilities lie within other teams. For people to work effectively together, to become more than a random group, they must share an understanding of their goals or tasks. They need to decide together on how they will achieve these purposes and understand each other's roles in this. The successful team also spends time reviewing how it is working, its own progress and functioning, and it celebrates its successes.

The pastoral team

We now investigate the particular contribution of the pastoral team to young people's learning, what is different about the pastoral team to other school teams, what function it performs for young people that is not provided by any other structure in the school.

First, the focus of the team is different. The pastoral team is committed to looking at the whole young person, not just their progress through the curriculum but their development towards adulthood. The focus is holistic. It takes account of the young person's personal, social, moral and spiritual as well as academic development.

Second, the pastoral team provides a structure to encourage teachers who have good skills to support young people, including listening and providing feedback and guidance for their learning. The team can be especially valuable in providing support and guidance for newly qualified teachers in their role as tutor. The team can work together to ensure that young people's pastoral care and entitlement is realized.

Third, the team can develop a coherent view about the young people's experience of school, especially if the team is organized around a key stage or a year cohort. They can help interpret this overall view to the young people and to their teachers. A creative team will search for patterns across their experiences that can contribute to their understanding of promoting learning. For example, they are likely to have a range of experiences of homework (setting, resources, completion, value, and contribution to learning, and links with parents) that will be available to enrich discussions. This richer knowledge and understanding of teaching and learning in the school can be represented to others whose view is only partial. In the case study, included later in the chapter, the observations from the quieter pupils gained from the individual Work Reviews are fed back to the teachers so they can alter what they do in the classroom.

Fifth, teams can provide support for each other's activities. For example, the head of year may complement the tutors' programme on learning about learning with Assemblies (see Chapter 4). Teams can share materials, plan programmes together, observe each other in tutoring conversations or in PSE lessons and review these activities together so that everyone in the team can learn from the experiences.

Pastoral teams can meet many difficulties in their work (see Calvert and Henderson, 1995). These can include several of the following:

- a lack of shared understanding in the school about what pastoral teams are for;
- this lack of shared understanding may be enhanced by poor communications;
- few teachers receive much training for their pastoral roles, and it is common for new teachers and pastoral team leaders to take up pastoral posts with no preparation;
- descriptions of the tutors' role and purpose are not common in schools – although a lengthy list of their responsibilities and tasks may be found;
- pastoral activities have less status than other work in schools;
- the particular stresses that can result from dealing with personal difficulties and crises may receive little recognition and the teachers may receive little care for themselves;
- teams may be struggling with resource differentials and difficulties with time, money, space and other resources;
- the most senior leadership of the pastoral system may not be adequate;
- accountability is often underdeveloped and lacking in structures such as baselines and benchmarks and lines of accountability.

Some of these difficulties can be a result of organizational arrangements which pastoral teams are not empowered to resolve but which must be tackled at a more senior level. Some difficulties that pastoral teams encounter may be to do with the team itself. The team members are unlikely to have been specifically selected, and many will not have commitment to the work of the team, or may find their personal resources overstretched and their priorities elsewhere. Team leaders often report that they find the hierarchical confusions in pastoral teams difficult to handle, especially if they themselves are young and inexperienced.

Individually, team members may find it hard to contribute as they or their fellow team members would like. They may be experiencing a very heavy workload and high levels of stress. They may feel a lack of strong commitment to this aspect of their work, especially if they feel they have not been properly prepared for it. They may feel that a lack of commitment from other team members makes their role more difficult. And they may feel that their role is unclear, or they may hold ideas about pastoral care that prevents them engaging in activities that supports students' learning.

The kind of difficulties outlined above have led some to ask whether the traditional structures of pastoral teams are the best way to support learning. Some schools have created Year Learning Teams (see Watkins, 1999) to address this. These teams concern themselves with curriculum matters and develop new understandings from the students' perspectives as well as particular concerns about non-learning. 'Schools experimenting with this structure have found it valuable to start working on issues which spanned the old pastoral–academic divide: examples include experience of pupil progress, patterns of homework, patterns of behaviour' (Watkins, 1999: 8). These teams are avoiding the 'pastoral–academic split' (see Table 7.1) and are creating teams of the key people involved in the tutor groups' learning.

Linking with the rest of the school

A theme of this book is that all the layers of the school need to work together to reinforce and complement each other's activities: tutor, classroom teacher, pastoral teams, whole school organization.

A key issue here is communications. Structures and relationships within the school need to support good communications about young people and their learning. These structures and processes need to include the young people, their parents and others involved in their learning. We discuss the tutors' networks in Chapter 4, and connecting with parents and others in the community in Chapter 6 and for young people whose learning is at risk in Chapter 3. In Chapter 9 we consider how the school can become a learning community so that its communications form part of the continuous feedback processes which are essential to organizational learning.

Pastoral teams are in a position to keep in touch with the changing context of schools, through their frequent contacts with young people and their parents. Schools need to respond both to internal and external pressures and contexts. It would be easy for the pastoral teams not to be alert to such changes because they are simply so busy. But these teams can act as both critic and reviewer of the school's responses to such changes in the light of how they are affecting young people's learning. For example, a year team analysed the range of subject teachers for each tutor group. One group had mostly newly qualified teachers and another all heads of departments. They fed back this information to the senior teacher responsible for timetabling and she was able to make some adjustments.

It is essential to keep an eye out for distortions in the school, and especially how the pastoral team is viewed by others. We often find versions of five distortions in our work with schools. These often reflect a lack of training in pastoral aspects of a teacher's role and something about the school and its view of education or its organization. Any one of these distortions described in Table 7.1 makes for less effective support of learning by the pastoral teams.

Table 7.1   *Distortions in pastoral care*

Distortion	
The pastoral–curriculum split	Tutors' and subject teachers' roles are seen as unconnected, rather than contributing to an overall goal. It is often more talked about than real as tutoring is part of being a teacher. It results from a lack of opportunity for teachers to communicate about students' learning, progress and their overall achievements.
Tutor–mentor split	Specialist mentors work with students in isolation from other teachers or tutors. Roles are seen as separate and unconnected, rather than contributing to an overall goal. We have seen examples of this split developing as part of Excellence in Cities projects and from careers advisers who are increasingly required to focus on learning, but have little connection with the teaching staff. This distortion also indicates a lack of opportunity for teachers and others to communicate about students' learning, progress and their overall achievements, and about the curriculum. In addition, the voice of the young people is excluded from the monitoring the process of mentoring.
The 'discipline' fixation – fire fighting	Pastoral staff are overengaged in responding to discipline problems, which have been referred by other teachers.[2] Little emphasis is given to developing positive control or to identification of the patterns of indiscipline and how they relate to curriculum, classroom climate, and relationships. In 1989 the Elton Report, *Discipline in Schools* (DES, 1989), recommended that all schools should develop behaviour policies, based on clear principles or values, worked out by all staff and involving governors and consistently applied by all staff. (See also Watkins and Wagner, 2000.)
Watered-down welfare	Hamblin (1978) called this distortion 'emotional first aid', where teachers exceed their roles, trying to solve problems of a small number of students and families. The school is ignoring the development needs of *all* students and taking a compensatory view of pastoral care.
Administrative overload	The school uses the pastoral system for administration: collecting the dinner money, and giving information to students. The Elton Report (DES, 1989) to the government on discipline in schools observed that the school caught up in this distortion needs to prioritize a focus on learning.

Each of these distortions requires some refocusing by the team. We now look at ways in which the team can develop this focus.

Developing the pastoral team

'Imagine that you would become a better teacher just by virtue of being on the staff of a particular school – just that one factor alone' (Little, 1990: 509). Most teachers have had the experience of being a better teacher in some schools rather than in others. We now pursue the idea that it is possible to be a better tutor in some teams than in others and ask you to imagine what would be required of the team for this to happen.[3] There are three broad categories: the team's focus, its external connections and its processes.

The team's focus

The team needs to keep the whole person in view, but to focus on their learning. This view of the young person must be set within a bigger picture that takes account of the conditions of learning (Rudduck et al., 1996).

The team's external connections

Teams that contribute to the effectiveness of each member will extend their vision beyond their tasks and their immediate colleagues. Members of the team create networks among the teaching staff, but they also see students and parents as partners in their work. In some schools we know they include the students when they refer to the year team. We discuss the tutors' network in Chapter 4.

The team's processes

We have already indicated that attention to the team's processes is important to make the team more than the sum of its parts. To help individual members become more effective tutors, pastoral teams need to clarify their goals, roles and contributions. Each individual needs to be valued for their strengths and contributions. The team that pays attention to its own processes will use dialogue to develop its understanding and develop a familiarity with talking about learning. In doing this the team will come to see itself as a learning team.

Here are some examples of activities that develop the team's processes that we have observed in schools we visit or had described to us by the practitioners.

Clarifying goals, roles and tasks

Clarifying the roles and relationships of team members can be a very useful learning process. Questions to help this process might include:

- What is the team here for?
- How are we going to achieve our goals as a team?
- What contribution will we make individually?
- Who has which skills and qualities in this team?
- In what ways do we think we are helping the year group with their learning?

These are the kinds of questions that can help the team and individuals clarify their roles within the team. Clarifying the tasks necessary to achieve team goals requires being explicit about team processes, which will help the functioning of the whole team (Lodge, 1999). Pastoral leaders, to whom we showed an early version of this chapter, agreed that they could see that it was important to do this very early in the life of their teams. They plan to discuss goals, roles and activities that promote students' learning in the first meetings of the team and focus less on administrative matters.

Working parties

By working parties we mean task groups, set up for the purpose of achieving a specific and time-limited task. We have come across examples of working parties set up to plan the personal-social curriculum and to plan an effective parents' evening or to work with the careers adviser on the planned programme for making choices about next steps. The value of this collaboration is that the team members work together to consider the issues, determine desirable outcomes, pool expertise and so forth. Limited responsibility can be given to less experienced team members, perhaps with the support of someone with more expertise.

Induction

Schools pay more attention than previously to the induction of newly qualified teachers, some provide induction programmes for teachers newly appointed to the school. Pastoral teams need to induct their new team members into both the practice but also the underpinning rationale for their work. Shadowing or co-tutoring with a fellow team member who is focused on helping students' learning is a useful strategy.

Observation and feedback

Professional learning can be greatly enhanced by observation followed by feedback that focuses on learning. This is likely to be feedback that involves the observer and the observed in a dialogue that avoids judgement (Watkins, 2000). Appraisal, in its most developmental form, can also provide constructive feedback. Visiting other schools to observe different practices and structures can also be useful.

Problem-solving

Teams often face problematic issues, especially about resourcing and space. The process of jointly solving such problems can lead to learning. However, a word of caution is necessary: meeting times that deal with practical and organizational issues can easily expand to take up all the available time. Teams that consider students' problems in learning will be fulfilling the pastoral teams' potential to enhance learning.

The pastoral leader

The role of the pastoral team leader is complex. The following is one head of year's reflections on how she and her team support the learning of the 210 students in their care. It illustrates the difficulties that are present in their school, but also the successes they have with handling data, monitoring progress and engaging in individual learning conversations with the young people.

Case study   The role of the head of year and the year team in supporting learning

Barbara Patilla, Mulberry School

I have always believed that I should review and evaluate the work I do in terms of the extent to which it supports or enhances a student's learning. One difficulty as a head of year is that out of the 210 pupils in my year group some pupils take up a lot of time in crisis management and attention-seeking behaviour. It can be difficult to keep the focus on learning.

My roles are many: dealing with conflict, monitoring attendance, checking progress, liasing with all other staff and parents and with outside agencies, overseeing dinner queues, developing the PSHE programme and playing a part alongside heads of faculties and the senior management team in the management decisions of the school. Reviewing the extent to which my time is effectively focused on supporting learning is itself a difficult task, but is essential to my learning and developing the role of head of year.

What are the strategies we employ to enhance the learning of pupils? As a head of year I have available to me all information known to the school about the pupils. This puts the whole team in a position to make decisions, in consultation with others, about the best ways to enhance pupils' learning.

For each pupil I keep *data records* on levels of achievement as they progress through the school. This includes other information about their learning such as scores from SATs at Key Stage 2, and reading and other assessments. For a head of year, as for any other manager in school, an effective database from which we can share and analyse information about progress of pupils and groups is essential for planning action to enhance learning.

Monitoring of progress is done biannually for the year group. Once a year there is a full report or profile for each subject which records all the levels of attainment and their progress – a summative document – with targets set or suggested by teachers. The pupil has their own page with comments on their progress and the targets that they have set for themselves. The tutor, head of year and headteacher also make comments on their progress and their contribution to PSHE, to the form and to the school. Finally the parents receive the profiles at a parents' evening and have a chance to talk to teachers and then write their own comments. The form tutor will see all the pupils and their parents. The headteacher and I will select some parents and pupils to praise and encourage their motivation to learn. At another point in the year, teachers are asked to complete a more simple record card for each pupil. This records information about their current attainment as well as their work in class and at home.

All of this information is valuable for tutors and myself to gain a picture of the progress of each pupil, identify individual concerns and highlight the achievement of students. More importantly, these records are useful to the pupils when they are reviewing how they are doing and to enable them to identify ways forward.

We have instituted individual *Work Reviews* of 15 minutes per pupil with their form tutor. These take place once a year but this needs reviewing and ideally should happen once a term. All form teachers have emphasized the importance of these reviews and have found them illuminating and useful for both participants. The value of the time spent with pupils in individual reviews cannot be overemphasized. They give value and importance to the individual and are a chance for teachers to get to know the individual pupil better. They are opportunities for raising issues about the factors in a group that enhance and hinder learning for the pupil. For example, some quieter pupils have explained the extent to which the more vocal and confident members of the class take up the time and attention of the teacher as well as affecting their concentration on learning.

Our first attempts at doing Work Reviews in this way have highlighted the importance of giving proper time to the reviews and of spending time developing the pupils' own skills in reviewing and learning and setting SMART targets.[4] These skills need to be developed from the pupils' entry to school and require much structure and practice.

There is much material available – particularly with the new Progress File (we have used Getting Started with the Year 9s) – but for this to be effectively used staff and pupils need time and practice. The time given by the school to Work Reviews is important. The tutors do not want pupils taken out of lessons or to have their lessons covered and it can be difficult to organize meetings after school. The evaluations of Work Reviews that I have experienced in my own school and seen in other schools indicate their importance in enhancing learning.

In focusing on the monitoring of progress as part of my role, I can see that I may have overemphasized the importance of levels of achievement in different subjects by pupils in my year group. As a head of year I am very aware of the importance of other aspects of the child's development, for example their social skills and confidence. Teaching is done in groups and the development of group ethos, which is trusting and supportive and enables all members to participate on an equal basis, is an ideal for all my classes. This ideal group would maximize the learning for all.

Mulberry School, London Borough of Tower Hamlets

Barbara Patilla's reflection on the team's work shows how hard it is for the year team and their leader to maintain a focus on learning. This team at Mulberry School has difficulties with the lack of time, which is common in all schools. Nevertheless, they have learned the value of working with data alongside the students, and engaging in learning conversations. These they have found very effective in helping the young people review their learning and identify possible next steps. This is the subject of Chapter 5. The case study is an example of the value of reflection, identifying a need to change the emphasis of the team's activities.

Another team leader led some action research with her team and this also led to important understandings so that she gradually changed her practice:

> I always thought change was rather technical. I focused on systems rather than people. I now realize the importance of working with teachers in a very personal way. As a team leader, for example, the way I relate to my team is very much based on thinking about how they are feeling, getting reports back from them on an almost daily basis. This seems to have increased their openness and confidence. It has altered the way I operate on a day to day basis. There hasn't been a huge change, but the small shifts are really important. (Head of department, reported in Carnell, 1999)

Research carried out by Eraut et al. (1998) suggests that the informal influence of the manager, as well as the micro-culture of the workplace is significant in professional development. They identified that one of the most important sources of learning was the challenge of the work itself and the interactions with others in the workplace. The role of the manager in professional development, they concluded, needs much more attention. The team leader can facilitate the interactions and to some extent control the extent of challenge in the workplace. We consider professional development more fully in Chapter 8.

Distortions in the pastoral team leader's role can develop just as they can within the pastoral system as a whole. They may develop a role with no connection to curriculum leaders and mentors, mirroring the pastoral–curriculum and tutoring–mentoring splits. They may become super-disciplinarians, 'fixing' a few individuals repeatedly. Or they may become super-tutors, taking on the tutor role for the whole student year group, or acting as welfare worker to a needy few. Barbara Patilla notes that a few young people make heavy demands upon her time. Reflecting the administrative overload, pastoral team leaders may retreat to their piles of paperwork or computers. These distortions are often responses to organizational pressures and distortions. Clarity about the role of the pastoral team and its leader is necessary at a school level, not just within the team. Finally, team leaders must pay particular attention to the needs of the other team members, of whom great things are expected from little investment by the school. This is sometimes called pastoral care for staff.

The pastoral team leader is expected, in difficult conditions, to ensure that the team is kept up to date with ideas and best practice in supporting learning and to look out for the development opportunities for the team and its members. For pastoral team leaders, according to Calvert (1998: 124), change is often 'messy, complex and fraught with problems and pitfalls'. Many pastoral managers will recognize this description, and it probably explains why many pastoral team leaders are only able to maintain rather than develop their teams. The advice to think big and act small, to keep chipping away but to keep the bigger view in mind, may be helpful. Reflecting on the work of the team, as Barbara Patilla and others have done, can help in maintaining the focus on learning, despite these difficulties.

Conclusion

There has been little written about the value of the work of the pastoral team in supporting young people's learning. This is strange when you consider that the endeavours of the subject team are widely promoted. The value of these activities for the members of the team is matched by the enhancement to students' learning. The pastoral team brings a varied range of experiences, skills and knowledge together in a holistic approach to the development and learning of the students.

Notes

1 The Teacher Training Agency published *Subject Leader Standards* in 1998, but it was left to NAPCE and the National Standing Conference of Inspectors, Advisers and Consultants for PSE (NSCOPSE) to relate these to pastoral leaders. See NAPCE (1999).
2 We are concerned that the government also appears to take this view of pastoral work in describing as 'pastoral' the programmes designed to help avoiding exclusions. This is a very old-fashioned view of the role of pastoral care.
3 We asked some pastoral team leaders at a NAPCE workshop on 'Managing Pastoral Systems' to imagine what the team could do to help tutors be more effective in supporting learning and we have used their answers to develop these ideas.
4 SMART targets are Specific, Measurable, Achievable, Realistic and Time scheduled.

Further reading

Best, R., Lang, P., Lodge, C. and Watkins, C. (eds) (1995) *Pastoral Care and Personal-Social Education: Entitlement and Provision*. London: Cassell.
Watkins, C., Carnell, E., Lodge, C., Wagner, P. and Whalley, C. (2000) *Learning about Learning: Resources for Supporting Effective Learning*. London: Routledge Falmer.

8

Teachers Learning about Learning[1]

This chapter considers the way in which schools can support teachers in their own learning about learning. We begin this chapter with a case study to illuminate a particular approach to teachers' learning. We argue this approach is more effective than other forms of professional development because it makes the teachers' learning visible and this has an immediate impact on young people's learning.

This chapter suggests the central learning themes of this book – being actively involved in learning, responsibility for learning, collaboration and meta-learning – are the same for teachers' learning as for young people's learning. This has consequences for the development of the school as a learning community, a focus for discussion in Chapter 9.

In the case study Peter Jarvis describes his work with two colleagues in bringing about change with young people in the classroom. These three teachers decide together on what aspects of their practice they want to make more effective, support each other in their changes over a period of time, involve young people in their learning and draw on theoretical perspectives to illuminate their work. These features characterize action research, a process of practitioners reflecting on and changing their own practice in order to make it more effective.

The discussion following the case study underscores particular themes:

- effective learning experiences for teachers;
- characteristics of learning teachers;
- shifting the focus from teacher development to teacher learning;
- the place of meta-learning dialogue in action research;
- supportive contexts for teachers' learning.

The case study demonstrates the connection between action research and professional learning. It explains how one teacher takes on the role of 'lead learner' and shifts the focus of activity from teaching to learning. Three teachers work collaboratively and develop meta-learning dialogue (see Chapter 1).

Peter Jarvis and his two colleagues work in an inner London comprehensive school. They decided to work with three Year 10 GCSE classes to introduce small group collaborative learning as a major part of the lessons. They wanted to test out the possibilities of making young people's learning more effective. This is an example of teachers shifting from a transmission model of teaching to a constructivist model (see Chapter 2). In their revised GCSE programme the three teachers encourage young people to take more responsibility for their learning, introduce more active and collaborative learning tasks and help young people focus explicitly on their learning.

Case study   *Improving practice through action research – an investigation into self-directed professional development*

Peter Jarvis   Ellen Wilkinson School, London Borough of Ealing

The planning process

I was very keen to test the possibilities of action research as a tool for professional development and to observe if it had possible positive effects in terms of school improvement. I realized I had recently been neglecting my pedagogy due to management priorities. The GCSE scheme of work had become rather one-dimensional. I consulted with the department and two colleagues agreed to participate in the research. We met as a departmental team of three and decided to conduct a collaborative review of a Year 10 scheme of work in an attempt to introduce more effective learning strategies. We devised a research programme for ourselves.

The initial meetings and action planning process were very interesting and we found we actually learnt more about ourselves as teachers than we thought would be possible in such a short time. I have been teaching for six years, five of those as head of department. Geoff has been teaching for 19 years and has a reputation for innovation and pupil-centred learning. John is only in his second year and is a little wary of innovation that might threaten classroom management. This mixture of experience helped to extend our learning as we were able to gain insights into the perspectives of other teachers at different points in their careers.

Initially the more experienced teacher, Geoff, was a little blasé about the overall effects that action research might have. He had experienced years of being 'reflective' and suggested this rarely produced real change. However, a discussion followed where I was able to draw on the idea of McMahon (1999) and argue that action research is not the same as being 'reflective'. The crucial difference according to McMahon is that action research involves 'strategic action' specifically designed to change and improve practice by gathering evidence. This was a powerful idea for Geoff who said it gave 'a greater rationale and structure for reflection and team working'. He became very interested in drawing up the programme and expressed a real sense of reinvigoration for the possibilities of new insights and for the collaborative nature of the programme.

The most fascinating and fundamental learning from these initial meetings came from the joint reading and discussion we had on the Watkins et al., (1996) publication *Effective Learning*. This helped us to locate our long-standing beliefs as teachers and to ponder the possibilities of breaking free from some 'implicit theories' (Claxton, 1996) we have carried for years.

We had to agree that our teaching had largely become based on the 'quantitative' conception of learning which emphasizes the transmission of knowledge as the key role of teaching. However, the reasons for this tendency to adopt this theory of teaching and learning differed. Geoff explained it by referring to feeling pressurized to deliver the knowledge within a second subject at GCSE. For John it was the pressure on a new teacher to ensure he delivered all the knowledge for the pupils for their examination. My explanation was similar but was expressed in terms of increasing pass rates at GCSE. What was clear was that we all felt pressurized to 'perform' and deliver knowledge. What we had neglected was any conception of developing pupils' learning skills beyond the pragmatism of the examination. This was a disturbing revelation for us that produced discomfort and some anger at a system that forces such narrow aims for education. We made a conscious decision to try to 'let go' and pursue a 'qualitative' conception of learning and attempt to produce a scheme of work that focuses on pupil action, collaboration, learner responsibility and, hopefully, meta-learning.

Research findings

Here I focus on two major questions – one related to teacher learning and one related to pupil responses to the action research.

1 What do our experiences as collaborative learners tell us about teachers' professional development?

I have already discussed some of the learning experiences we went through in terms of understanding our 'implicit theories' of learning and how the research project attempted to deliberately challenge these. The agreed scheme of work also required us to 'break our own rules' (Head and Taylor, 1997) by using small group collaborative classroom arrangements that we were not used to. Geoff was concerned about the tight structure of the learning process and expressed doubts about its practicality. John was concerned about the group work element and the required change to classroom arrangements, his fear being that this may lead to a worsening of pupil behaviour. I needed to 'let go' of the learning and let pupils direct their own learning process without continual interference. Interestingly, after a week we all felt that our fears were being realized and had we not been working collaboratively we may well have gone back to our old methods. However, in the meeting after the third week of the research it was really interesting to discover that we had all softened our attitudes and were beginning to see the benefits of the innovation. Certainly this seemed good evidence to suggest that teacher learning is enhanced by collaboration through the support and encouragement of others to do the things that ordinarily we may avoid.

The meeting and the diaries we kept provided a wealth of information on the personal responses to the collaborative learning process. What became clear was that the outcomes and processes identified by Watkins et al. (1996) as being indicative of 'effective' learning for pupils were being replicated in terms of the learning experiences for teachers.

The comments that came from teacher diaries and meetings suggested:

– deepened knowledge:

- I understand more fully how pupils learn.
- It has increased my understanding of how I learn.
- I've learned more about how to help pupils make progress and the usefulness of more group work.

– positive emotions:

- I've enjoyed the whole process – it's given me a lift.
- I've really enjoyed working as a team.
- I have found the responses of pupils really rewarding and exciting.

– enhanced sense of self:

- It has made me feel more positive about the relationship I have with the pupils; helped me refocus and feel what I am doing has a real effect.
- It has given me a personal focus and some much needed intellectual stimulation.
- Despite my initial worries it has convinced me that I am a good teacher as the pupils responded so well.

– connection with others:

- I have really enjoyed the chance to talk through the ideas with others and come up with new ideas.
- As head of department I think we are now more of a team that ever before; the effect I think will be long lasting.
- I have found the collaborative aspect of the research very rewarding and good for an old hand like me to be shaken up now and again.
- The teamwork involved was crucial for the learning; we were ready to quit after a week!

– changed meaning and experience:

- I definitely have a changed understanding of the ways pupils learn and how I work.
- The view I have of group work has been transformed; it is now not a means to an end but an end in itself.
- I feel more confident in playing a part and knowing that more experienced staff will value my views.

– making connections about learning in different contexts:

- I can see that our learning is reflected in the work we have developed for the pupils.
- In some ways it is obvious that if pupils are 'doing' the research method they will learn more effectively; you usually do learn more from doing than just reading about it.

– reflecting about one's own learning strategies:

- I have learned that I probably do learn better within a group though I would never have thought it before.
- I have enjoyed this project and learned a lot; I know that effective learning takes some attempt to involve practical application, even if it is just talking it through with a friend!
- I have learned that you are never too old to learn.

I am convinced that the overwhelmingly positive response to the action research project was in some part due to the feeling of collegiality it engendered. For a large percentage of our time as teachers we operate in isolation and the collaborative nature of this project allowed for intelligent discussion on issues and an exciting chance to come out of our isolation and work towards a collective goal.

Another factor that became apparent was the enthusiasm generated by the opportunity to plan, direct and carry out a piece of relevant research. It would seem the self-direction and agency this allowed in terms of self-development created a very positive and creative environment. Indeed, both teachers involved have expressed an interest to volunteer to take part in another project next year. I found this slightly surprising as the research process did without doubt create extra work. They said they had no objection to extra work as long as the time involved was productive and beneficial.

2 What do pupils' responses tell us about action research and an understanding of teachers' professional development?

The evidence from pupils falls into two categories, the teachers' observations from lessons and pupil written responses. Interestingly two teachers reported some initial resistance from the pupils to the change in the working environment and activities. On reflection this was not surprising and in following lessons pupils began to respond positively to collaborative structures. Again a lesson here may be to persist with a change for a while.

Overall we all found the pupils responded positively to the opportunities to work together and share their learning. Indeed we all noticed a more mature attitude from most pupils and a greater engagement with the set tasks. An interesting element of the continued pair work and small group work was the effect it had on the pupils in terms of their relationships. The pupils' prior knowledge that they would work together in small groups for the next four weeks led to the development of what Anderson (1999) terms 'relational responsibility'. It engendered in them an understanding of their responsibility to their group and I believe acted as a positive motivational factor.

The pupil responses to the evaluation exercise provide much evidence to support the claims made by the teachers:

(a) Have you enjoyed working together? Explain your answer.

- Liked the chance to discuss.
- Not at first but I got used to it, I feel more confident now.
- Liked having to decide together.
- I said things that I would not say to the class.

(b) Do you think that working in groups helped your understanding? Explain.

- Listening to other people sometimes I thought 'Oh yeah'.
- I definitely got ideas that I would not have got on my own.
- Yes as I had to read all the work.
- I liked being able to look at other people's work.

(c) Do you think you have learnt anything about yourself?

- I work better with others.
- Speaking to my friends helps me understand.
- I am not good at talking in front of the rest – but getting better.

(d) Do you feel confident about carrying out the course work?

- I think I will do it better now 'cause I understand it.
- I think I could do good in-depth interviews.
- I still need help but I think I know the basics.
- Having the aims at the start of it all makes sense.

(e) Any other comments?

- Some people do not speak enough.
- I think the teacher should teach more!
- I'm bored of keeping discussing.

As some of the final comments show, a change in learning styles can be uncomfortable for pupils and may even lead to a teacher questioning the value of their method. Consequently this may possibly lead a teacher to return to the transmission model of teaching which feels safer in terms of teacher activity.

In attempting to summarize what I have learned from the pupil responses I would argue that teachers' professional development should perhaps attempt to focus on ways of developing teaching/learning styles that promote pupil motivation based on what Dweck (1986) terms 'learning orientation'. Unfortunately, our education system seems to be increasingly obsessed with performance and accountability which tends to foster the dependency 'performance orientation' and professional development reflects this.

Closing thoughts

Despite the small scale of the piece of action research it has had very positive effects: it has brought the department together; it has reinvigorated our interest in searching out methods for pursuing our core values as teachers; we have gained important insights into our 'implicit theories' of learning and how they affect our teaching styles; we have learned more about ourselves as learners and the power of collaboration in generating a learning community; and, lastly, despite the fact that we have no concrete evidence yet, I do believe we have improved our practice. All this achieved during seven weeks of strategic action research to improve classroom practice. We all agreed that this has been one of the most powerful professional development experiences we have undertaken.

Ellen Wilkinson School, London Borough of Ealing.

What we find most striking about Peter's case study is the way it demonstrates how action research as an approach to teachers' learning encourages a learning community. We now discuss the elements which enable teachers to bring about changes to professional practice.

Effective learning experiences for teachers

This case study confirms other research findings about effective learning experiences for teachers (see Table 8.1). 'Effective' is used in the sense of bringing about change to professional practice.

In investigations with teachers an interesting pattern emerges. Teachers say they experience more of the less effective forms of professional development. These include:

- passive, didactic experiences, where there is an overreliance on external expertise;
- external directives;
- one-off training events.

These experiences may result in a quick fix but they do not often result in lasting change and may, in fact, be counterproductive (Carnell, 1999).

The less effective forms of professional development are of low complexity – the 'one size fits all' model. They are usually short term, individualistic and context free. They are single-track, usually focusing on content or skills and do not require judgement. The more effective forms are of high complexity. These take into account the teacher's experiences and emotions and are dependent on particular learning and social contexts. They are multi-track, meaning they focus on and connect different aspects of the context,

Table 8.1 *Effective learning experiences for teachers*

Effective learning experiences for teachers:

- are linked inextricably with their day to day work contexts, for example, in the classroom or working with groups of colleagues in their school

- are challenging, developmental and take place over an extended period of time

- arise when teachers feel in control, have ownership, develop shared aims and reciprocity – supporting and being supported by respected colleagues

- are participatory; the more teachers are engaged in activities and the more interaction with colleagues, the more effective the activities are seen

- are practical and relevant with opportunities for reflection, learning and change

- happen in a trusting, non-hierarchical environment

- include pupil and peer dialogue

- occur when teachers work together in social exchange, reflecting, planning and developing actions for change

- focus explicitly on their own learning.

Source: Carnell, 1999

develop understanding, facilitate learning and change. They require reflection, analysis, judgement, dialogue and collaborative responsibility for learning. These factors are vital in providing the necessary conditions for actions for change: 'At its best, professional development helps teachers understand their school and contribute to school-based improvement efforts' (Watkins and Mortimore, 1999: 13).

From these discoveries it appears that professional development and the learning context are most usefully seen as linked.

Characteristics of learning teachers

One way of analysing the case study is to consider the characteristics that might describe 'learning teachers' (see Table 8.2).

The evidence from the case study shows how these teachers are enhancing their learning. Particularly striking is the way in which they take risks by trying new ideas in the classroom and asking young people for their views. The teachers use a number of challenging strategies, for example, keeping a learning diary and using theoretical readings as a focus for dialogue. The disclosure of how they would have abandoned the experiment provides evidence of the power of collegial support groups in maintaining learning and change.

The case study demonstrates the importance of taking account of feelings in any situation involving change. Making the emotional effects explicit in learning conversations is more likely to strengthen the teachers' resolve in bringing about change. Understanding that other colleagues had reservations and were anxious about the changes seemed to have an appreciable effect on

Table 8.2   *Characteristics of learning teachers*

Learning teachers…	Explanation
Have a lifelong commitment to learning and change	This commitment is evidenced in teachers' willingness to take risks and promote new ideas. There is concern to seek out ways to improve professional growth, including evidence of a system for continuous, inquiring and complex decision-making. Learning teachers keep up with professional knowledge and new conceptions; they grow personally as well as professionally.
Collaborate with young people and colleagues	Learning teachers create collaborative working relationships with students and colleagues. They are able to maintain collegial support groups and manage the classroom in collaboration with students. They are able to demonstrate reciprocity, self-disclosure and mutual respect.
Have a commitment to increasing the effectiveness of teaching and learning	This commitment is exhibited in their strong motivation to be involved in things they care about, their ways of creating more adaptive ways of teaching and learning and in their ability to reflect and understand assumptions, beliefs, and values. This commitment includes understanding and respecting the diversity of their students.
Have an holistic, multi-perspective view of teaching, young people and relationships	Taking an holistic view of teaching and learning requires seeing students as whole human beings. Understanding interactions and the impact of interactions upon one's self and others is important as is self-knowledge and the ability to think critically. Teachers who take an holistic view exhibit empathy, flexibility and high levels of humane and democratic values, appreciate multiple possibilities, multiple perspectives and interdependency of relationships. They encourage complex learning.

Source: Carnell, 1999

their willingness to take risks. There is an important connection between feelings, purposes and effects.

Perhaps the most notable feature in the case study is the way the teachers were encouraging complex learning both for themselves and for young people by focusing on learning itself. This process is more than reflection, which Geoff was sceptical about, but to do with strategic change leading to 'a real sense of reinvigoration for the possibilities of new insights'.

While the case study is positive in tone we should note that the three teachers had to deal with their own reservations as well as the reactions of their students to the changes they introduced. Spending time anticipating possible blocks and problems is a useful strategy. When changes are introduced there may be a period of discomfort for all involved as people deal with unfamiliar and unexpected outcomes. Benefits from changes can be slow to emerge. They may also be small scale or hard to discern.

Shifting the focus from teacher development to teacher learning

Collaboration, co-construction, dialogue, on-the-job learning and support emerge from the case study as vital in effective learning. Colleagues see themselves as collaborative learners who, through their own learning, create conditions to make young people's learning more effective. This illustrates that the way teachers view learning matches a congruent approach to professional development. In the case study the teachers see themselves as professionals, capable of creating their own agendas for professional development, addressing issues related to decision-making, practice and professional knowledge about learning (Blackman, 1989). This is a high-complexity approach and is very different from a competence-based, functionalist view where managers of schools or government provide the agendas of professional development (Blackman, 1989). In the functionalist view the focus is on what the teacher can do, rather than what the teacher is, and can become.

We draw on a model to demonstrate how the approach to teachers' learning taken in the case study differs fundamentally from other forms of professional development. The model is formed using two continua – from objective to subjective and from individual to collective (see Figure 8.1). By considering professional development along two axes, objective–subjective and individual–collective, we can identify four approaches. These four approaches are:

- didactic;
- co-operative;
- empowering;
- community.

Each of these four approaches implies a different emphasis in its purpose and focus and the control of the process (see Table 8.3).

We suggest the case study is an example of professional learning of the 'community' approach. This perspective challenges the low complexity of learning in the didactic approach because the didactic approach favours individual, cognitive development rather than collaborative, holistic learning.

The idea of belonging to a learning community changes the way we think about teachers' learning:

> Its importance lies in the fact that it changes the relationship of teachers to their peers, breaking the isolation that most teachers have found so devastating. In supportive communities, teachers reinforce each other in a climate that encourages observing students, sharing teaching strategies, trying out new ways of teaching, getting feedback, and redesigning curriculum and methods of instruction. (Lieberman and Miller, 2000: 58)

The case study illustrates changing relationships at two levels. Not only do relationships change between teachers and teachers but also between teachers and young people. The changed relationship described by Lieberman and Miller above can be seen in the case study, but there is another dimension

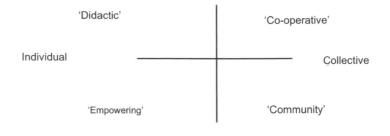

Figure 8.1   *A two-way continuum of planned professional development experiences (Carnell, 1999)*

Table 8.3   *Four approaches to professional development*

Didactic
- Fundamental purpose: bringing about change through analysis of individual needs and directing teachers' action
- Focus: individual achievement through the acquisition of knowledge and skills
- Control: decisions made by 'experts' about individuals' needs

Empowering
- Fundamental purpose: bringing about change through individual, personal development and facilitating individual development
- Focus: individual improvement through understanding
- Control: decisions made by individuals about their own needs

Co-operative
- Fundamental purpose: bringing about change through analysis of organizational needs, based on external demands
- Focus: organizational achievement through the application of knowledge and skills
- Control: decisions made by 'experts' about the organization's needs.

Community
- Fundamental purpose: bringing about change through collective, whole organizational development
- Focus: organizational development through collaboration
- Control: decisions made collectively about the needs of the organization.

which has a greater transformatory power. Here is a sense of learning together by talking about their *learning* not their teaching, engaging in *co-constructive conversations* rather than traditional forms of feedback which focus on performance (Watkins, 2000). This we describe as developing a meta-learning dialogue, that is, dialogue which focuses on learning about learning (see Chapter 1).

The place of meta-learning dialogue in action research

An analysis of the case study shows how a meta-learning dialogue can develop. Three stages emerge: talking about learning; using action research and learning diaries to learn from experience; reflecting and learning about own learning.

Stage 1: talking about learning

In the case study, the teachers use a theoretical text to trigger discussion about learning. They develop a learning vocabulary and differentiate between different perceptions of learning. For example, they discuss the difference between reflection, learning and strategic action. They also discuss possible changes to their classroom practice to make young people's learning more effective.

Such discussion indicates that learning cannot be assumed to be happening without making it explicit. There needs to be a specific focus on learning about learning, what is learned, how learning takes place, and how that learning can shape future practice. Learning, as opposed to reflection, is a conscious and deliberate change (see Figure 8.2). By focusing on the elements at the meta-level learning becomes explicit.

Stage 2: using the learning cycle to learn from experience

In the case study the teachers use learning diaries to monitor their learning and then together draw on them to analyse their experiences. They meet together regularly to talk about their experiences and to reflect on their changes. As we saw in the case study, application of learning may not be automatic, immediate or easy. The teachers would have given up the experiment if they had worked alone.

The importance of such dialogue taking place in a supportive climate cannot be overestimated. Reflecting on experience allows opportunities to examine strategies for keeping safe, acknowledging the difficulties of 'unlearning' old patterns and 'letting go' of established and safe structures. The learning dialogue they created kept them going by recognizing the many different dimensions of learning and change.

Stage 3: using the learning cycle to reflect and learn about own learning

The action learning cycle can be used in a reflexive manner to examine participants' own learning – the process then becomes a meta-learning process. Watkins et al. (1996) explain how this occurs (see Table 8.4).

The changes brought about by action research can be considered at a meta-level, requiring reflection on the learning.

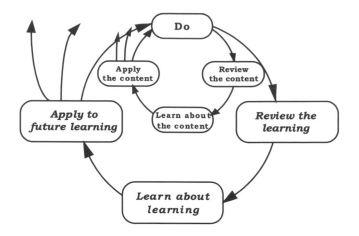

Figure 8.2   *A meta-level learning (Watkins, 2001)*

Table 8.4   *Promoting learning about learning*

Do: using particular learning tasks, attention is focused on learning

Review: learners evaluate the process of learning they have gone through. This includes affective as well as cognitive aspects, that is, how emotional aspects help or hinder the learning

Learn: a range of aspects may be identified and learners' strategies compared

Apply: each learner identifies learning situations in which they wish to try out new strategies and approaches.

The following prompts show how meta-level learning might be achieved:

● What am I learning about the way I respond to change?
● What am I learning about the way I respond to disappointments and others' reactions?
● What am I learning about how the context supports or inhibits me?
● What am I learning about patterns in the way I learn?

In action research the researcher is not normally expected to use the process as a meta-learning opportunity. This is a richer conception of professional learning and of action research than is usually held (Carnell, 1999).

Supportive contexts for teachers' learning

The case study shows how innovations at school level can occur when an individual or small group becomes enthusiastic about trying out new ideas. Initiatives such as small-scale action research projects need to be harnessed within the wider school context. But the way in which initiatives are introduced is crucial, as professional learning is more likely to be powerful in its engagement if teachers have constructed their own narrative of the need for change (Rudduck, 1991a). In the case study we see an important link between effective transformation, ownership of the initiative and positive emotion. Coercion can be counterproductive.

Teachers may find it difficult to bring about actions for change if the internal conditions of the school are not conducive (Rosenholtz, 1991) and if teachers are not involved in goal-setting and decision-making and the collegiality of group learning (Bell and Day, 1991). Some forms of collegial work are more effective for learning than others (Little, 1990). For example, weaker forms of collegial work include

- storytelling;
- providing help and assistance;
- sharing resources and ideas,

whereas stronger forms of collegial work include

- team teaching;
- observations, feedback and dialogue;
- action research;
- mentoring;
- joint planning, design and evaluation of teaching materials.

In the case study Peter Jarvis and his colleagues were involved in the stronger forms of collegial work such as action research, joint planning and evaluation. Not included in Little's examples are the specific ways Peter Jarvis and his colleagues focused on learning through dialogue around literature and on meta-learning conversations about the changes to their classroom practice. We think these are even stronger forms of collegiality as they help develop learning communities by providing structures which develop 'learning teachers' and focus on learning.

These stronger forms of collegiality are mentioned by Munro (1999: 155) as part of a set of necessary conditions for teacher change. In the case study each of the following conditions Munro identifies are being met:

- learning through active constructive processes;
- valuing existing implicit knowledge about learning;
- framing goals or challenges for learning;
- engaging in collegiate collaborative activities;
- engaging in self-direction and systematic reflection of their practice;
- exploring and demonstrating new teaching procedures in their classrooms.

As in the case study, Munro's research suggests that systematic exploration of the learning process, with teachers developing their knowledge of learning, has a direct impact on effective teaching and on teachers' personal explicit theory of learning.

Rather than individual teachers or small groups of teachers engaging in action research and meta-learning, we develop the idea of a whole school approach for learning in the next chapter. In a whole school approach 'the research community becomes the central focus, while the school culture itself becomes the context for collaborative efforts' (Aspland et al., 1996: 93). This has the potential for developing research approaches which are empowering and have value as professional development experiences:

> It suggests new types of communication amongst teachers; dynamic networks of relationships to assist them in taking responsible action in the face of complexity and uncertainty. This kind of collaboration implies exchange processes among teachers or between teachers and other groups in which there is a symmetry, rather than an hierarchy of power. (Altrichter et al., 1993: 202–3)

Examples of small-scale research where teachers are learning together through strong forms of collegiality and are engaged in meta-learning dialogue, such as the one we have featured in the case study, can demonstrate to colleagues a sense of continuous learning for teachers being a norm of the school.

Concluding comment

This chapter suggests that research and professional learning can be one and the same enterprise; a phenomenon that can be practical and emancipatory for all participants (Day, 1991). The teachers in the case study became more aware of the complexity of learning as a realization of the complexities of their own behaviour, motives, relationships, reactions and blocks, and of the complex contexts in which they work. The teachers moved from the intuitive to the explicit. A sense of empowerment experienced and acknowledged by the teachers demonstrates the 'emancipatory potential' of action research (Smith, 1993).

The teachers' learning was developed through meta-learning dialogue. In this expanded perspective of professional learning teachers:

- recognize themselves as learners;
- use that learning-centred spirit to transform schools into learning organizations;
- reassert their own moral autonomy to provide space and time for serious, reflective thought and study (Sockett, 1996).

Sockett calls this a redefinition of teacher professionalism and suggests it needs to be extended to include headteachers. This is like Barth's (1990) suggestion that head*teachers* be known instead as head *learners*.

Drawing on Stenhouse's (1975) vision of teachers integrating research into their practice, Aspland et al. (1996: 101) suggest: 'It is everyone associated with schools who, in the end, will change the world of the school by understanding it critically, collaboratively and transformatively.' Through meta-learning dialogue generated from action research teachers create conditions to make their own and young people's learning more effective. Aspland et al.

emphasize the involvement of *everyone* and in our next chapter we consider 'schools for learning' which is about everyone being part of a learning community.

Note

1 This chapter is an extended version of an article: Carnell (2001).

Further reading

Altrichter, H., Posch, P. and Somekh, B. (1993) *Teachers Investigate their Work: An Introduction to the Methods of Action Research.* London: Routledge.

Claxton, G. (1996) 'Integrated learning theory and the learning teacher', in G. Claxton, T. Atkinson, M. Osborn and M. Wallace (eds), *Liberating the Learner: Lessons for Professional Development in Education.* London: Routledge.

McNamee, S. and Gergen, K. (eds) (1999) *Relational Responsibilities: Resources for Sustainable Dialogue.* Thousand Oaks, CA: Sage Publications.

Watkins, C. (2000) 'Feedback between teachers', in S. Askew (ed.), *Feedback for Learning.* London: Routledge Falmer.

9

Schools for Learning

Every morning young people leave their homes and families and cross the school boundary to enter different buildings and to spend their day with other young people and adults. They are entering organizations characterized by diversity, discontinuities and complexity of time, space and relationships. The buildings may be arranged on more than one site, or in unconnected blocks. The day is broken up into units of about an hour and its many interruptions do not relate to the way in which many individuals learn. In the curriculum the young people must negotiate a whole series of separate traditions and discontinuities of subject matter.

The young people have to manage a diverse range of social relationships, and keep learning how to do this as they and their fellow students mature, and this maturity affects both their relationships with their peers and the adults in the school. Classrooms are complex places (Doyle, 1986) as was discussed in Chapter 2, and young people must learn to negotiate these and learn the differences between classrooms. They need to learn and understand the culture of the school, its unspoken rules, its hidden curriculum. Within this shifting and complex context young people have much to do to find their way to learning. Their learning can get lost or made more inaccessible by the intrusion of organizational or bureaucratic matters, and by relationship issues. This chapter considers how the school can become a learning community. We have considered the individual learner, how the class teacher and tutor and their teams can support the learning of young people. Here we look at the level of the whole school.

We use the term *learning community* because there is a very real sense in which all members of the school community need to learn together. In a learning community, the important ends are the growth and development of the people. The means are the ways in which community members work and learn together. This is in contrast to a learning organization where the ends are organizational growth, productivity, efficiency and effectiveness. The people and the learning they do in support of organizational goals are the means in organizational learning (Mitchell and Sankey, 2000). In a school it is the growth and development of its members which are important. It is quite hard to resist the idea that output (measured in test results) is the purpose of schools in the current policy climate, however.

We have described three models of learning in Chapter 1 and referred to them throughout this book: the reception model, and the constructivist and the co-constructivist models. It is the latter, with its emphasis on collaboration and dialogue that is most likely to support the learning community. Schools that are successful at promoting the learning of all their members are building learning capacity. Communities that learn are doing the following:

- making effective learning visible;
- measuring and tracking effective learning;
- encouraging new ideas through experimentation and boundary spanning;
- sharing values that promote effective learning;
- promoting people who are effective learners;
- creating a setting that encourages learning (after Ulich et al., 1994).

These activities are significant in that they focus on how the structures of the organization are used and on the nature of relationships which support learning. This chapter considers these relationships and structures by considering in turn the following aspects of learning communities:

- relationships that enhance learning;
- structures in learning communities;
- two case studies;
- promoting a learning community in a school;
- factors which hinder and promote a learning community.

Relationships that enhance learning

Relationships between teachers and other adults, and the young people are significant in promoting a learning community. They can be fostered and encouraged by the school structures and processes. We have already considered in detail the role of the class teacher (see Chapter 2) and that of the tutor in supporting learning (see Chapters 4 and 5). In the following examples we show how the school can promote relationships between teachers and students that can influence learning.

The first example relates to both a process and its outcome, taken from a book concerned with self-evaluation in schools. The list describing 'the good teacher' was drawn up by a group of Year 8 girls. The teachers in the school generally acknowledged that it was fair, insightful and offered a good checklist for self-evaluation (MacBeath, 1999). Our main purpose in presenting this example is to describe a simple process that can promote discussion between young people and their teachers about relationships in learning.

Example   The good teacher:

- is kind;
- is generous;
- listens to you;
- encourages you;
- has faith in you;
- keeps confidences;
- likes teaching children;
- likes teaching their subject;
- helps you like their subject;
- takes time to explain things;
- helps you when you're stuck;
- tells you how you are doing;
- allows you to have your say;
- makes sure you understand;
- helps people who are slow;
- doesn't give up on you;
- cares for your opinion;
- makes you feel clever;
- treats people equally;
- stands up for you;
- makes allowances;
- tells the truth;
- is forgiving.

Source: MacBeath, 1999: 60

This rather idealized list of characteristics of a good teacher reflects students' appreciation of supportive, trusting, patient and enthusiastic attitudes by the teachers. It is closely connected to the requirements of the Year 10 students, reported in Chapter 1, who want responsive teachers. This means teachers who take account of student needs, who make an extra effort to make themselves available and who have enthusiasm for their subject. There can be no escaping the emphasis on the interpersonal in these descriptions of learning relationships.

As MacBeath (1999) points out, teachers and students do not exist in a vacuum but are influenced by one another's expectations and behaviours. Mutual discussion about expectations and behaviours can lead to increased understanding about teacher–learner relationships that promote learning. Explicitness about what is valued in teachers and learners encourages a learning community. A process that invites dialogue about what it means to be members of the community, to be a learner, a teacher, what are good lessons, for example, can promote self-review at an individual and organizational level. The good teacher, described above, has relationships with students that are based on trust, openness and they therefore allow this kind of self-review process to take place.

The second example has a very different feel. It is from a school in which one of us worked, where hierarchical beliefs imply very different relationships between teachers and students, relationships that lack warmth and trust and are characterized by a desire to control.

> *Example*
> Teacher to Year 10 student: You don't behave like that in my classroom.
>
> A notice on the front entrance written by the caretaker: PUPILS NO ENTRY! USE THE SIDE DOOR.

In this example the pupils are regarded as being in inferior positions, are being told that they have little ownership of their school and can only contribute with permission. This reflects the observation (in Chapter 2) that the classroom can be seen as the teacher's territory. In some very real ways the school in this example was closed to its pupils and to learning from them or with them.

The third example is of a teacher–student relationship and is characterized by a lack of belief in seizing the opportunity to take up students' interests and initiatives, or to explore an important question.

> *Example*
> The boy in an RE lesson on Jesus' miracles asked if miracles happened today. This sparked a real interest in his peers yet he was hushed up immediately by the teacher 'because you haven't finished the worksheet yet' (Curtis, 2000).

Completion of task comes before the interest and potential learning of the class. Schools that encourage a focus on performance may find that teachers develop relationships with students that require them to avoid risk, accidental discovery and unintended learnings.

Schools may find it easier to influence teacher relationships and their culture than those of their student group. In a learning community the students support each other. In some schools students are abused by other young people as 'swots' or 'boffs' and seen as uncool. In learning communities students see the value of supporting each other's learning and can be explicit about it, as the next example shows.

> *Example*
> A Year 7 student replied to a question about why she liked helping others in her class by saying, 'You learn more, because if you explain to people what to do, you say things that you wouldn't say to yourself really. So you learn things that you wouldn't know if you were just doing it by yourself' (Lodge, 1997).

In the learning-oriented culture relationships are focused on learning (Bentley, 1998). In a chapter entitled 'Nurturing Learning Relationships' Bentley describes how these relationships depend on one overall principle: mutuality. Mutuality requires openness and sensitivity and so attention has to be paid to emotional and social aspects of the school, and to learning about relationships within the curriculum. Fostering such learning relationships is a challenge for the school because 'for learning relationships to work, they must be reciprocal' (Bentley, 1998: 168). Reciprocity here means more than mutual respect. It includes acceptance of difference, of challenge and a shift in the power relationships between teacher and student. At times, the student is accepted as the leader, as the teacher and as the learner. This challenges hierarchical traditions in schools. As we have seen from the examples, such relationships are based on trust and openness, and support for risk-taking and experimentation. Mutuality also means making the most of relationships that may extend beyond the boundaries of the classroom or the school. They may be supported by new technologies such as cyber-relationships, e-mail, mobile phones, video links and so forth.

In the learning community it is the relationships that activate the purposes of the community, ensuring that learning is visible and explicitly valued, and that success, achievement and progress are celebrated by all. Relationships alone are not the full story. Structural arrangements are needed to support them and we now consider these.

Structures in learning communities

Making learning visible is crucial to developing a learning community. This means making learning the object of attention, of conversation, of reflection and of learning itself (Watkins, 2001). In learning schools the organizational structures reflect the school's long-term commitment to learning and change. Leadership and management provide support for risk, experimentation and evaluation by creating structures that:

- foster collaborative learning cultures among young people and teachers, by creating learning teams and encouraging dialogue – see for example Year Learning Teams and Circle Time, described later in this chapter;
- increase the effectiveness of learning for teachers through professional development and a focus on learning about learning;
- encourage continual discussion about learning that encourages an approach which is complex, has multiple perspectives and takes an holistic view of young people;
- develop learning dialogues with young people and adults (see Chapter 1).

These activities, at a whole-school level, embody the themes that we have been discussing throughout this book: activity in learning, collaborative learning, responsible learning and meta-learning.

The benefits of the learning community come directly to teachers and to the students. We consider these benefits in turn. Kruse et al. (1995) describe the benefits to teachers of developing what they call a 'professional community'. They identify increased efficacy for teachers through an increased sense of affiliation to each other and to the school, enhanced mutual support and individual responsibility and increased opportunities to improve practice through feedback and appreciation. They identify five characteristics of such communities, see Table 9.1. Four of these require teachers to talk and learn together, and the fifth indicates the focus of their communication.

Table 9.1   *Characteristics of professional communities*

1. Shared norms and values
2. Reflective dialogue
3. Public discussion of practice
4. Collaboration
5. Focus on student learning

Source: adapted from Kruse et al., 1995

In professional communities, the teachers spend time with each other exploring their own practice, reviewing and learning from this collaborative approach, always focusing on the learning of the students. In Chapter 8 we consider a case study where the teachers' meta-learning leads to collaborative learning. Such communities have to be nurtured through structural arrangements and supported by the cultural elements of the school, discussed below. This includes how the organization of the school helps and hinders their learning through arrangements such as the following:

- time to meet and talk – for example, scheduled team meetings;
- physical proximity – for example, teams of teachers being based in the same area;
- interdependent teaching roles – for example, employing teachers who offer more than one subject and who are committed to tutoring;
- good communication arrangements – for example, using voice- and e-mail and providing meeting space;
- teachers being empowered – for example, making decisions about the syllabus and learning materials;
- a degree of autonomy for the school – for example, in the appointment of teaching staff.

It follows from these structural arrangements that the cultural aspects of the learning community must include supportive leadership, relationships characterized by trust and respect and openness to improvement. They also include access to expertise from within the school, and also from outside it. A finding of the study of professional communities also identified the importance of opportunities to socialize in building the culture for learning. These cultural elements are, of course, interlinked with the structural ones. We can see how they help make learning visible, span boundaries, help share values to create a setting that encourages learning.

Such learning communities are not common, but many schools contain elements, or achieve a temporary sense of community. There may be temporary or small learning communities within a school: we describe the creation of one in the case study in the previous chapter, where three teachers created a small community. Circle Time can provide a temporary learning community for a class or tutor group, as we see in the following case study.

Two case studies

The benefits to the students of the learning community are related to our four themes: learner responsibility, activity in learning, collaborative learning and meta-learning. Schools differ in how far they hear and respond to the voice of the students. In some schools, evaluative comments by students of lessons and planning with students for the next session are routine. In some schools, School Councils or Circle Time is used to involve young people in the organizational learning processes. The two case studies consider how some schools have developed elements of a learning community.

Case study   Developing Circle Time in Harrow Secondary Schools

Moya Brewer

> I think circle time in school is a good idea, because it can help get rid of stress and makes you feel better about yourself for listening to other people. (Year 9 student, Rooks Heath High School)

In transition

Harrow's primary schools have, for a number of years, embraced Circle Time, from adopting the whole model and incorporating it into school behaviour policies, to individual teachers using Circle Time sessions for 30–60 minute slots with their classes. It was a group of Year 8 students in one of the high schools who spoke directly to their head of year and asked for Circle Time in their secondary school: it was something they missed when they transferred at the end of Year 7.

Simultaneously, members of the Access and Development Team (Behaviour Support), who worked across both primary and secondary phases, recognized that transition could be difficult for students and that Circle Time could provide a bridge at this stage in the pupils' lives. They felt that group building with new classes in secondary schools would be enhanced if Circle Time became a feature of PSHE and tutoring programmes. Circle Time has a structure and provides a supportive listening system with which pupils in middle school were familiar, but their secondary teachers were not.

What is Circle Time?

Circle Time is a democratic and creative approach used to consider a wide range of issues affecting the whole school community. It involves a whole class, including the teacher, meeting in a circle at least once a week to look at issues related to personal, social, and health education. Its structures encourage positive relationships, self-discipline, self-regulating behaviour management, conflict resolution and assertive communication. It also encourages skills of thinking, observing, listening, speaking and concentrating (Mosely and Tew, 1999).

Gathering data

Pupils in their final year at primary school (Year 7) completed a questionnaire about their experience of Circle Time in primary schools. It showed that in some Harrow schools 93 per cent of pupils had experienced Circle Time, and over 80 per cent had valued that experience. This data supported the plan to pilot Circle Time in 1998–9. A working group of a Year 8 school curriculum co-ordinator, an educational psychologist and two behaviour support teachers met regularly. They set up a network group for colleagues to support those piloting the model and to provide opportunities to share good practice, exchange ideas and to demonstrate aspects of the model. INSET in host schools was provided for individual teachers and teams. The initiative was supported by the LEA's recognition of the contribution Circle Time can make to raise self-esteem, so it was included as a key priority within its Education Development Plan for 1998–2002.

Developing the model

From 1999 Circle Time has been included by a number of Harrow secondary schools in their student induction programmes and a few have planned to extend Circle Time to Year 9 cohorts who have experienced it as part of their Year 8 PSHE programme. Developmental work with colleagues and students is exploring other aspects of the model, for example one-to-one Talk-time, or Drop-in Time, Think Books and Year Council frameworks.

Secondary PSHE through Circle Time

One secondary school has involved all its Year 8 tutor team in delivering all aspects of its PSHE programme through Circle Time and has continued this with its Year 9 programme. A number of Year 10 and Year 11 tutors run regular Circle Time sessions to sort out issues, needs and challenges which arise within their tutor groups. The school has committed a full day's INSET with all its staff to Circle Time, with sessions facilitated by Marilyn Tew. Its successful OFSTED inspection report highlighted the use of Circle Time:

> Teachers are willing to adopt new methods, especially when pupils have benefited from them in middle schools. Recently the personal, social education programme has been improved by the use of Circle Time . . . This is unusual in secondary schools and is a good example of teachers' willingness to maintain good practice started elsewhere. The pupils respond well, offering comments and displaying high levels of mutual trust and support. Social education is a strength of the school. (OFSTED Report, 1999)

Networking

Harrow has made a commitment to ongoing professional development and continues to support schools through network group meetings that take place twice termly in different schools, and offers twilight, whole- and half-day INSET for year teams and schools throughout the academic year. Harrow also supports in-school training and it is included in the LEA's programme for newly qualified teachers' INSET. This developmental approach means that Circle Time is becoming part of secondary school teachers' practice.

I was unfamiliar with the model and concerned I would do it wrong. What I discovered was that my knowledge was of little consequence, the students themselves had all the expertise having been taught to use Circle Time so well in middle school. The students were keen to start using Circle Time again. They had clearly found it a valuable experience. (Head of drama and tutor)

Work in progress video

Many of these developments in Harrow have been recorded on a video that shows Circle Time session in progress and includes interviews with students and teachers. Their comments represent the highs and lows of this way of working.

The video was used at the New Directions in Behaviour Support Conference in September 2000. It formed the basis of an interactive session with a range of colleagues, who were impressed that this democratic listening system had so easily translated into a secondary school setting, and with the partnership between schools and the LEA in developing it as a transition vehicle between phases of schooling in Harrow.

Circle Time sessions made me feel welcome when I joined the school later than everyone else. (Year 8 student, Rooks Heath High School)

The impact of Circle Time

Tutors have also been positive about the impact on their own classroom teaching of Circle Time. Commenting on the improved relationships among the students one teacher said 'it makes teaching PSHE enjoyable'. 'I like the atmosphere it creates in the classroom. It gives everyone the opportunity to speak, even the quiet ones,' said another teacher.

It has enabled students and teachers to plan together, to reflect together and to problem solve. One Year 8 group took nearly a year to become a cohesive class. They reviewed their first year at secondary school using Circle Time to speak, listen and agree their action plan as a class. The power of this way of working emerged during the summing up as it demonstrated the learning and the increased understanding they now had of each other to build on in the following year.

At the start of Year 8 we used not to get on and to go on at each other . . . we need to respect each other as we want to be respected. (Year 8 students, Rooks Heath High School)

Access and Development Team (Behaviour Support), Harrow

In this study of the development of Circle Time in Harrow secondary schools we note a number of significant features related to the development of a learning community. We note that in introducing Circle Time the schools went beyond their individual boundaries to work together and with LEA personnel. In looking at how to assist young people with the transition between school phases, strategic knowledge was sought, from the students and those experienced in Circle Time. The introduction of Circle Time has encouraged problem-solving and experimentation. These are features of learning communities, in this case a community that involves schools and others from across an LEA. Circle Time has also created temporary small-scale communities in some of the classrooms, helping young people to create better learning relationships and conditions.

Other significant features that are aspects of learning communities include:

- students collaborating with each other and with the teachers;
- empowerment of young people in their own experiences;
- responsiveness to students' requests;
- building on previous knowledge, especially that of the students;
- openness to adopting good practice from elsewhere;
- recognition that time to talk and listen is important;
- trust and support developing between teachers, and with students;
- embedding new practices into structures and procedures such as school and LEA development plans;
- schools' and LEA's commitment to supporting teachers through multi-disciplinary team meetings and professional development days.

In our second case study Polly McLean describes the unusual practice of meditation in two schools. While it refers to younger students, there is no reason why some of the benefits and processes may not apply to older students.

Case study   Meditation

Polly McLean

In 1999 I made a study of pupil and teacher perceptions of the effects of meditation on learning in two primary schools where meditation is practised. Sunrise is a very small independent school (approximately 35 pupils aged 5–11) in North London, run by a worldwide socio-spiritual organization. Here meditation was a core part of the school's philosophy and was practised as part of Circle Time each morning. Cheddar First School is a state school with 250 pupils (aged 5–9) in a small Somerset town. At this school meditation took place at a voluntary lunchtime 'Peace and Quiet Club' set up by one teacher enthused by his own meditation practice and supported by the headteacher. Meditation was also used occasionally in assemblies and as a precursor to creative writing classes.

   Meditation is a practice that can take place within a secular as well as religious context. It is fundamentally a regular practice undertaken for the sake of inner peace. Basic meditation is most frequently practised by sitting quietly and bringing the mind to a single focus, one's own breath, a candle or an internally repeated word or phrase (mantra). Another popular kind of meditation, used in both schools, is guided visualization. Here meditators similarly sit quietly, usually with their eyes closed. The teacher or other facilitating person then prompts them to visualize an imaginative journey in which they visit a place of calm and beauty and receive a gift of wisdom. Both types of meditation, with primary children, would usually last for 15–30 minutes. In both cases the intention is for the mind to focus one-pointedly, not to be distracted by daydreams or worries, and thus attain alert calmness.

Both schools valued a perception of learning which involved 'changing as a person' (from Marton et al., 1993; see also Chapter 1) as shown by this comment:

> What we're really trying to do is support children in becoming, or staying, whole integrated people, who are aware of all or as many parts of themselves as possible . . . we hope they're going to go and become effective people in the world, with positive relationships. (Founder of the Peace and Quiet Club, Cheddar School)

Congruent with this is the strong emphasis placed by both schools on the affective and social as well as cognitive development of their pupils.

Benefits for pupils

Perceptions of the impact of meditation on learning and development were observed in three main categories: readiness for learning, enhanced creative expression and spiritual development.

1 Readiness for learning

The main impact that teachers commented on was that meditation quietened the pupils down. A pupil at Sunrise school said 'it probably does help us because we're not so . . . excited during the day . . . [without it] we might be more . . . talkative and more difficult'. This role of meditation is reflected in the name 'Peace and Quiet Club'. The headteacher suggested that this quietness developed in meditation improves pupils' listening skills, enables them to communicate better and allows them to pay greater attention to visual information. It is not quietness itself that is valued in these schools, rather the ability to be quiet and calm when necessary and this is seen as conducive to learning, including collaborative learning.

> Children that ordinarily found it difficult to sit still, and who were often regarded as quite disruptive in the classroom, came . . . and could and were able to keep still in those circumstances. (Founder of the Peace and Quiet Club)

Indeed, it was this physical calmness of the pupils that was commented on by the OFSTED inspector who attended a Peace and Quiet Club session at the school.

A second perceived benefit concerns the ability to handle distractions and cope with pressure, as in the following example:

> I did have one child say that . . . he used to get bothered by other children making noise around him . . . but he'd found that since coming . . . he wasn't being affected in the same way, and that he found it easier . . . to shut out distractions and concentrate on what he was doing. (Founder of the Peace and Quiet Club)

All the teachers interviewed in the study commented that meditation seemed to help pupils' concentration and helped them focus on their work. Although they speculated that this would aid academic performance they were aware of the difficulties of proving that link. Perceptions of this benefit are also supported by Mann's research (1995). Mann conducted meditation classes with one class at secondary school, using another class not taking part as a control group. She found that although the research group's academic performance in general was not substantially affected, they did outperform the control group on one occasion when an exam took place in stormy weather under difficult and distracting conditions. Meditation seems to support learning by providing pupils with a resource for coping with pressure and stress.

2 Enhancing creative expression.

Teachers interviewed at Cheddar School said that the guided visualization meditations before creative writing classes greatly enhanced the quality of pupils' writing. The school's OFSTED inspection report supports this perception:

> Meditation . . . makes a significant contribution to the quality of education and the pupils' personal and social development . . . the pupils' attainment is above average and they make good progress, particularly in the development of descriptive writing. (OFSTED, 1998)

The headteacher suggested that guided visualization 'does heighten . . . their awareness of things'. Similarly the founder of the Peace and Quiet Club understood the role of meditation for creative writing in terms of motivation – that guided visualization can be a 'marvellous stimulus for creative work . . . as a teacher you're always looking . . . to give children a reason for writing'.

3 Spiritual development

Meditation at Sunrise School was taught primarily as a spiritual practice, enabling pupils to become more aware of themselves and their common humanity. Likewise, the headteacher of Cheddar School claimed that the Peace and Quiet Club and the guided visualization meditation helped children to develop 'an awareness of the world around them, their place in it, the beauty around them . . . the sense of wonder'. This corresponds closely with the School Curriculum and Assessment Authority's (SCAA's) description of spiritual development as including 'a sense of awe, wonder and mystery – being inspired by the natural world, mystery, or human achievement' (SCAA, 1995: 3). The evaluation of awe and wonder is problematic but it seems that OFSTED found them at this school.

Benefits for teachers

The sense of calm and coping easily with stress was noteworthy among teachers at the two schools. They were able to give substantial time and attention to the interviews and were actively interested in discussing educational innovation. All teachers attributed their calmness to their own meditation practices. One teacher at Sunrise School said:

> It's a spiritual life that certainly allows me to . . . cope with my many roles where I work and many demands in my very active and busy life. I feel very privileged . . . really where I work, and my future.

Meditation may be a means for teachers to engage in systematic reflection as a support for their own learning.

Meditation in schools

It would appear then that meditation is potentially a valuable practice for schools. Teachers' enthusiasm was not matched by the pupils' who were unable to say much more about the meditation than it was relaxing and seemed perplexed by questions concerning the relationship of meditation to learning. One way to help pupils understand this relationship would be to encourage discussion and reflection, following a session, as part of the *Do, Review, Learn, and Apply* cycle (see Chapter 1).

   The current emphasis on accountability and assessment runs the risk of favouring those subjects and activities that are easily assessable and squeezing out those that are not. Although meditation has potential for affective, social and cognitive learning, it must be admitted that it is not assessable. But meditation could form part of the provision for pupils' spiritual development.

   Meditation can have a profound and positive effect on school ethos and attitudes to learning. A growing number of schools are using meditation to support cognitive, social and affective development. The size of sample in this study makes it impossible to generalize from the findings, or to draw parallels or differences across phases of schooling. It is hoped, however, that it will provide food for thought, discussion and innovation.

See also McLean (2001)

The examples of schools working with meditation are undeniably outside the mainstream. However, we included them because they illustrate a number of features of a learning community.

- They are innovative and take risks.
- The leadership is supportive of innovation.
- Practice is connected to aspects of learning and the school is alert to this.
- Meditation provides an ideal setting for reflective practice.
- There is an unusual example of one teacher who has connected his own spiritual life to that of his pupils.

In these case studies the schools have encouraged a setting that is conducive to learning. They have used the relationships, structures and processes of the schools to develop learning communities that benefit their students. We now look at what school leaders, managers and governors can do to promote a learning community.

Promoting a learning community in a school

It would be a mistake to take the earlier description of the learning communities and to treat them as prescriptions. Schools are unique and each needs to engage in self-study before considering what action to take. Schools that are learning communities have developed relationships, processes and structures that promote organizational learning. By this we mean that the school learns how to achieve its purposes more effectively through relationships, structures and procedures that ensure problems are identified and solved. This idea of organizational learning is becoming increasingly common outside education, in the world of business and commerce (Reed and Stoll, 2000; Senge, 1990). In practice the functions of learning by the people and learning by the organization are inseparable because the organization does not exist separately from the members of the community.

Reed and Stoll have identified four processes which managers need to employ to promote a learning community:

- working actively with context;
- creating, processing and using strategic knowledge;
- developing learning-oriented cultural norms;
- thinking systemically (Reed and Stoll, 2000).

We now take these in turn and consider their practical implications for school leaders and managers.

Working actively with context

Schools do not operate in isolation from each other, or from their context. Learning schools have permeable boundaries, filtering out influences that do not benefit the learning of young people. This is what is meant by 'encouraging new ideas through experimentation and boundary spanning' (after Ulich et al., 1994) quoted at the start of this chapter. We refer the reader to Chapter 6 for more on linking students' learning with their context. Organizational learning takes account of context, especially for the development of strategic knowledge, to which we now turn.

Creating, processing and using strategic knowledge

Strategic thinking, in contrast to incremental improvement, looks further ahead to possible, but not defined futures. Strategic thinking means starting with the long-term view. Learning schools engage with their communities to determine what kinds of students the community wants to see the school producing in 10 or 20 years' time. They ask what contribution does the community want to see the learning school making to the development of young people. Other knowledge is sought from experts, both within and outside the school, that is, people who are thinking about what learning might be like in the future, what knowledge and skills might be essential, the implications of the interacting changes to our world and the implications for schools. This creation, processing and use of strategic knowledge is a continuous process in which all teachers are involved.

Developing learning-oriented cultural norms

The culture of a school is the embodiment of beliefs and values generally held which are referred to as norms. In the learning school, norms that are learning orientated dominate the culture. These schools make learning the object of attention, of conversation, of reflection and of learning itself. There are four norms that are particularly significant and we look at these in turn:

1 Collegiality among teachers.
2 Problem-seeking and solving.
3 Acceptance of risk and experimentation.
4 Feedback is welcomed.

We have considered the importance of collaborative learning and its special significance in co-constructive learning for all members of the community. Collaboration, rather than competition or individualism, imbues the practices of the learning school at all levels. At the whole-school level, active partnerships give attention to the voices of all stakeholders in working towards the goals of the school. Teachers particularly contribute to the development of this norm, through collaboration and co-construction which integrates personal and professional learning (as in the example of the teacher who introduced meditation to Cheddar School), maintaining the focus on learning and through action research. The interconnection of these levels of understanding – personal, organizational, theoretical and practical – creates a powerful base when linked to collaboration, co-construction, relational responsibility, learning about learning and action research (see Chapter 8).

A second norm is that the school constantly seeks and solves problems. Processes to do this are active, promote collaborative learning, and encourage responsibility in learning and engagement in meta-learning. To understand this cultural norm let us consider a common scenario and different responses in two schools.

Example
In one school, the majority of students in one class have been referred to their tutor for failing to complete their homework. The tutor explored the pattern a little more closely by identifying where the complaints came from and, by talking with the students concerned, she discovered that the complaints all relate to science and to a particular kind of task which required additional resources at home, which these students did not have. She informed the teacher of these difficulties, and the homework tasks were adapted and additional resources made available. The complaints reduced.

> In the second school the tutor was also receiving complaints about failure to complete homework, but she kept the children in after school to complete it. As the resources were available the homework was done, but the problem recurred every time this kind of homework was set.

The response of the first tutor produced learning for the organization, the response of the second merely allowed patterns to be repeated.

A third norm is the acceptance of risk and valuing experimentation as in our two case studies related to Circle Time and meditation. Learning schools encourage experimentation and provide a zone of security which allows for mistakes and wrong turnings (Clarke, P., 2000). There is a greater need for creative thinking, at individual and organizational levels, at this time of rapid change than there has ever been. But in a climate that encourages compliance and certainty this can be hard to encourage in schools.

> Risk is one of the undiscussable aspects of improvement because it inevitably implies unknown territory to be crossed, with no plan and no idea of where the journey might lead . . . It is a vital feature of a learning school that it will take risks in order to survive. Risk implies conflict, disagreement, disorder, and an amplification at times of inconsistent actions amongst staff. The alternative is not to take risks, to apply overarching consistencies through applied vision and values and plans. (Clarke, P., 2000: 137)

Although often very uncomfortable and difficult to manage, embracing risk is necessary in order that communities can learn. In order to do this schools need to provide the necessary conditions: 'Time for experimentation, trial and error and handling failure are essential parts of learning. They symbolize a willingness to try something different, to consider new approaches, and to move into uncharted territory' (Reed and Stoll, 2000: 132).

A fourth important cultural norm is that feedback is regarded as significant for identifying problems and minimizing the undesirable effects of risks taken. This engagement in feedback takes place at individual, student and teacher levels as well as at organizational level. For teachers working together in teams it means team teaching, mentoring, action research, peer coaching, planning and mutual observation and feedback by teachers, and teamwork to develop whole school aspects, and these are associated with support, mutual respect, openness, celebration and even humour. In the homework example described above, it also relies on communicating significant information among teachers. This communication is important in setting the climate or culture. (See Askew, 2000: pt III.)

Feedback from the students, on all aspects of school life, is heard in the dialogue of the learning school. This is promoted through active school councils and Circle Time. But we go further and suggest that students need to be heard in reviewing individual lessons and the curriculum (MacDonald, 2000), in dialogue with teachers about what makes a good teacher (see above) and a good lesson. A range of strategies for eliciting the feedback and promoting this dialogue can be found in *Schools Must Speak for Themselves* (MacBeath, 1999).

Thinking systemically

The fourth key process for managers to develop is thinking about the school in a systemic way, that is, looking at the whole as well as the parts and their connections. It is the opposite of reductionism, which is the idea that something is simply the sum of its parts. A collection of parts that do not connect does not make a system. Many schools do not function as systems by this definition. 'Breaking a whole into parts is analysis. You gain knowledge by analysis. Building parts into wholes is synthesis. You gain understanding through synthesis. When you take a system apart and analyse it, it loses its properties. To understand systems you need to look at them as wholes' (O'Connor and McDermott, 1997: 59).

Learning communities look beyond the immediate to find patterns over a wider spectrum or longer period of time. They encourage feedback to identify problems and successes. This kind of thinking gives them some measure of control over their future and their preparations for it (O'Connor and McDermott, 1997). In this book we present a systemic view of learning in the secondary school. We have considered each level of learning, the individual, the classroom, teachers and the organization as a coherent system. This system is effective when it achieves its purpose of promoting the learning of the young people.

All these processes – working actively with context, thinking strategically, developing learning-oriented norms and thinking systemically – involve teachers in dialogue amongst themselves and with their students about teaching and learning. In Gray et al.'s longitudinal study the researchers noted how only a small number of schools appear to be able to build capacity to improve effectively at the 'learning level'. It was just this focus on learning that marked out the two schools that were successful in promoting improvement. 'They had developed ways of being more specific about precisely how they wished to improve pupils' learning, were able to draw on colleagues' experiences to formulate strategies and had found ways of helping colleagues evaluate and learn from their own and other teachers' classroom experiences' (Gray et al., 1999: 146). These schools had gone beyond tactical and strategic thinking to develop a capacity to change.

We now consider some of the factors that hinder and some that promote the capacity to develop learning cultures.

Factors which hinder and promote a learning community

It is a sad truth that not all schools promote learning. Indeed some schools contribute to the difficulties young people have in engaging with learning (see Sally Wells's case study in Chapter 3). It is also a sad truth that in many schools members of the school community do not see their purpose as promoting learning. We have worked in schools where the needs of the teachers took precedence. One of us has worked in a school regarded as an important source of childcare by parents who demonstrated this by sending younger siblings to school with their older children, when they had childcare difficulties. Schools' custodial function for society as a whole determines some of the arrangements we make about school, especially by providing childcare while parents are working (Hargreaves, 1995). While these are not common examples, they do illustrate the point that it can be hard to concentrate on promoting learning when members of the school community do not see this as the central function of the school.

Even where schools are seen as primarily places of learning, different groups want young people to learn for different purposes, and what they want them to learn is often disputed. Currently the government believes that learning is the key to the country's economic success: 'Learning is the key to prosperity – for each of us as well as for the nation as a whole . . . To achieve stable and sustained growth, we will need a well-educated, well-equipped and adaptable labour force' (DfEE, 1998: 7). Others believe that the purpose of schooling is to help young people get a job. Still others talk about schooling as being about personal fulfilment. Still others see schooling as being about all these and yet more. As with individual learning, organizational learning can benefit from spending time in dialogue and clarifying purposes in learning and then reviewing their progress and difficulties in achieving them.

There are three particular difficulties for schools in developing a learning community. The first is that the organization and structures of schools determine how teachers teach, how students learn and the nature of the relationship between adults and young people in schools. These divisions of time, students and the curriculum are so embedded that it can be hard to innovate (Cuban, 1993). An example of this is the so-called 'pastoral–curriculum divide' which exists in many schools. It will be clear from Chapter 7 that pastoral teams can provide a great deal of support for young people's learning, enhancing the contribution of individual teachers and tutors. However, in many schools the pastoral and curriculum functions are unconnected and uncoordinated. Watkins has argued that building Year Learning Teams can connect and co-ordinate the two teams' functions. He reports that in schools which are trying out using learning teams the teachers work in more collaborative ways and 'they show more integrated ways of talking about pupils, with the focus on learning rather than on the split perspectives of the past' (Watkins, 1999: 8). Experimenting with new structures and relationships, then, may help overcome learning blocks within the organization.

The second difficulty is that schools are overwhelmingly concerned with the immediate and day-to-day activities of teachers and learners. Schools are busy places. Often a thousand people are engaged in many different tasks in any one day, or at any one moment. It is a place of myriad interactions, of continuous interaction. Not all of these interactions are comfortable, joyous or developmental. They can create problems in the school, which need immediate attention and are often resolved with the smooth-running of the organization as the primary aim. To use every incident as a learning opportunity is very time-consuming. Some schools get locked in patterns of repeated behaviours and need to consider how to improve school behaviour (Watkins and Wagner, 2000). A sustained focus on the immediate takes attention away from strategic thinking about learning. This is as true at an organizational level as it is at the individual level.

The third difficulty is that schools seem less and less able to act independently to promote the learning of their youngsters. Over the last 15 years schools have been increasingly subjected to legislation, inspection, resource-led initiatives and other mechanisms by which central governments have pursued their agendas. While much of what has been achieved as a result of this centralized pressure is to be celebrated, the climate within which secondary schools now operate is constrained, and may work against schools promoting learning for its students or its organization. The climate of accountability which surrounds our schools make it less likely that our most timid school leaders will do other than comply with the pressure to demonstrate improved performance. The consequences of failure make it harder to take risks. We have frequently commented in previous chapters that a focus on performance will depress learning and may not improve performance, while a focus on learning will enhance both learning and performance.

These difficulties make it hard to promote schools for learning. Yet there is a considerable force for change within our schools, especially among the teachers and the young people. Schools and schooling are the focus of a great deal of political activity and, at last, of improved resourcing. In the last few years there has been a shift to more of a focus on learning within schools, and more recently among those who influence policy at local and national level. Research and the literature on school improvement is focusing on the need to create schools that have the capacity to develop a learning orientation (Stoll, 1999).

Conclusions

We began this chapter with a list of activities observed in learning organizations (Ulich et al., 1994). We end this chapter, and this book, by describing how these activities can be encouraged within a school. In the Introduction we describe our vision of learning schools that support effective learning. Each chapter elaborates on a different aspect of this support, and here we draw them together as a reminder of the connected nature of these activities.

In learning schools individual learners are encouraged to become active, responsible, collaborative in their learning, and aware of their purposes, feelings, strategies and contexts. Teachers and schools can help them develop meta-learning strategies to make sense of their experiences, to embrace complexity and the values that promote effective learning (see Chapter 1). In learning schools classrooms are rich learning environments. Learners are engaged in challenging tasks involving them in dialogue, assessing their own learning and using feedback. Effective learning is made visible. Classroom activity promotes the language of learning. Teachers encourage learners to become less dependent (see Chapter 2).

To support those most at risk in their learning these schools bring people together to pool their resources. They meet different needs differently by taking an holistic approach (see Chapter 3). To support all young people's learning these schools develop connections between parents, teachers and others in the community, spanning the school boundaries. The school adapts its organization to promote these connections (see Chapter 6).

Tutoring is encouraged and developed as a key role for supporting learning. Tutors help the young people to connect their learning across the curriculum and to learn about learning (see Chapter 4). The school organizes regular and frequent individual learning conversations featuring the *Do, Review, Learn and Apply* cycle which includes a meta-learning focus. Effective learning is measured and tracked (see Chapter 5). The pastoral teams take account of the personal, moral, spiritual and academic development of young people, providing a structure for feedback and guidance (see Chapter 7).

Learning schools encourage teachers to be learners themselves through research and constructing new ideas through experimentation. They listen to young people's feedback (see Chapter 8). The school's relationships, structures and routines support learning at every level. Effective learners are celebrated (this chapter). All these activities create a setting that encourages and supports learning. Our vision, then, is of a learning school that is a place where people want to be together, want to learn together, are excited together and feel powerful together.

Further reading

Bentley, T. (1998) *Learning Beyond the Classroom: Education for a Changing World.* London: Routledge.

MacBeath, J. (1999) *Schools Must Speak for Themselves: The Case for School Self-Evaluation.* London: Routledge Falmer.

Reed, J. and Stoll, L. (2000) 'Promoting organisational learning in schools – the role of feedback', in S. Askew (ed.), *Feedback for Learning.* London: Routledge Falmer.

Watkins, C., Lodge, C. and Best, R. (eds) (2000) *Tomorrow's Schools – Towards Integrity.* London: Routledge Falmer.

Further Information

Readers can obtain further information from the following organizations, which were mentioned in the book.

NAPCE
National Association for Pastoral Care in Education
c/o Institute of Education, University of Warwick
Coventry
Warwickshire CV4 7AL.

Meditation
Gina Levete
The former Meditation in Education Network
14 Carroll House
Craven Terrace
London W2 3PP.

Circle Time
Quality Circle Time
Jenny Mosely Consultancy
8 Westbourne Road
Trowbridge
Wiltshire BA14 0AJ
Website www.jennymosley.demon.co.uk

References

Altrichter, H., Posch, P. and Somekh, B. (1993) *Teachers Investigate their Work: An Introduction to the Methods of Action Research.* London: Routledge.

Anderson, H. (1999) 'Collaborative learning communities', in S. McNamee and K.J. Gergen (eds), *Relational Responsibility.* Thousand Oaks, CA: Sage.

Askew, S. (ed.) (2000) *Feedback for Learning.* London: Routledge Falmer.

Askew, S. and Carnell, E. (1996) *School, Home and Professional Networks.* Bristol: Avec Designs Ltd.

Askew, S. and Carnell, E. (1998) *Transforming Learning: Individual and Global Change.* London: Routledge.

Askew, S. and Lodge, C. (2000) 'Gifts, ping-pong and loops – linking feedback and learning', in S. Askew (ed.), *Feedback for Learning.* London: Routledge Falmer.

Aspland, T., Macpherson, I., Proudford, C. and Whitmore, L. (1996) 'Critical collaborative action research as a means of curriculum inquiry and empowerment', *Educational Action Research,* 4 (1): 93–104.

Baird, J. (1986) 'Improving learning through enhanced metacognition: a classroom study', *European Journal of Science Education,* 8 (3): 263–82.

Barber, M. (1996) *The Learning Game: Arguments for an Education Revolution.* London: Gollancz.

Barber, M. and Graham, J. (1994) 'That critical first year', *Times Educational Supplement,* 23 September (2): 5.

Barnes, D. (1986) 'Language in the secondary classroom', in D. Barnes, J. Britton and M. Torbe (eds), *Language, the Learner and the School.* Harmondsworth: Penguin.

Barth, R. (1990) *Improving Schools from Within: Teachers, Parents and Principals Can Make a Difference.* San Francisco, CA: Jossey-Bass.

Bell, L. (1992) *Managing Teams in Secondary Schools.* London: Routledge.

Bell, L. and Day, C. (1991) *Managing the Professional Development of Teachers.* Milton Keynes: Open University Press.

Bennett, A. (2000) *Father! Father! Burning Bright.* London: Profile Books.

Bentley, T. (1998) *Learning Beyond the Classroom: Education for a Changing World.* London: Routledge.

Best, R. (1999) 'The impact of a decade of educational change on pastoral care and PSE: a survey of teacher perceptions', *Pastoral Care in Education,* 17 (2): 3–13.

Best, R., Lang, P., Lodge, C., & Watkins, C. (Eds.). (1995). *Pastoral Care and Personal-Social Education: Entitlement and Provision.* London: Cassell.

Betterton, H. and Nash, J. (1996) *Academic Tutoring: Developing the Process.* Sutton: Secondary and Further Education Services.

Bigge, M.L. (1982) *Learning Theories for Teachers.* New York: Harper Row.

Biggs, J.B. and Moore P.J. (1993) *The Process of Learning.* Englewood Cliffs, NJ: Prentice-Hall.

Black, P. and Wiliam, D. (1998) *Inside the Black Box.* London: School of Education, King's College, University of London.

Blackman, C. (1989) 'Issues in professional development: the continuing agenda', in M.L. Holly and C. McLoughlin (eds), *Perspectives on Teacher Professional Development.* Lewes: Falmer Press.

Broadfoot, P., James, M., McMeeking, S., Nuttall, D. and Stierer, B. (1988) *Records of Achievement: Report of National Evaluation of Pilot Schemes to the DES by the PRAISE Team.* London: HMSO.

Brookes, J.G. and Brookes, M.G. (1993) *In Search of Understanding: The Case for Constructivist Classrooms.* Alexandria, VA: Association for Supervision and Curriculum Development.

Brown, A.L. and Campione, J.C. (1998) 'Designing a community of young learners: theoretical and practical lessons', in N.M. Lambert and B.L. McCoombes (eds), *How Students Learn: Reforming Schools through Learner-Centred Education,* Washington, DC: American Psychological Association.

Bruner, J. (1996) *The Culture of Education,* Cambridge, MA: Harvard University Press.

Budge, D. (2000) 'Just one more piece of paper', *Times Educational Supplement,* 20 October: 25.

Bullock, K. and Jamieson, I. (1995) 'The effect of personal development planning on attitudes, behaviour and understanding', *Educational Studies,* 21 (3): 307–21.

Bullock, K. and Jamieson, I. (1998) 'The effectiveness of personal development planning', *Curriculum Journal,* 9 (1): 63–77.

Bullock, K. and Wikeley, F. (1999) 'Improving learning in Year 9: making use of personal learning plans', *Educational Studies,* 25 (1): 19–33.

Bullock, K. and Wikeley, F. (2000) *The Evaluation of Personal Learning Planning for Cambridgeshire Careers Guidance.* (Summary.) University of Bath and University of London.

Calvert, M. and Henderson, J. (1995) 'Leading the team: managing pastoral care in a secondary setting', in J. Bell and B.T. Harrison (eds), *Vision and Values in Managing Education: successful leadership principles and practice.* London: David Fulton.

Calvert, M. (1998) 'Managing change in pastoral care: a strategic approach', in M. Calvert and J. Henderson (eds), *Managing Pastoral Care.* London: Cassell.

Calvert, M. and Henderson, J. (eds) (1998) *Managing Pastoral Care.* London: Cassell.

Carnell, E. (1999) 'Understanding teachers' professional development – an investigation of teachers' learning and their learning contexts'. Unpublished PhD thesis, Institute of Education, University of London.

Carnell, E. (2000) 'Dialogue, discussion and feedback: views of secondary school students on how others help their learning', in S. Askew (ed.), *Feedback for Learning.* London: Routledge Falmer.

Carnell, E. (2001) 'The value of meta-learning dialogue', *Professional Development Today,* 4 (2): 43–54.

Carnell, E. and Lodge, C. (2000) *Tutoring for Learning.* Coventry: NAPCE.

Cassidy, S. (2001) 'Children becoming upwardly mobile', *Times Educational Supplement,* 2 March: 12

Clarke, P. (2000) *Learning Schools, Learning Systems.* London: Continuum.

Clarke, S. (2000) 'Getting it right – distance marking as accessible and effective feedback in the primary classroom', in S. Askew (ed.), *Feedback for Learning*. London: Routledge Falmer.

Claxton, G. (1996) 'Integrated learning theory and the learning teacher', in G. Claxton, T. Atkinson, M. Osborn and M. Wallace (eds), *Liberating the Learner: Lessons for Professional Development in Education*. London: Routledge.

Claxton, G. (1999) *Wise Up*. London: Bloomsbury.

Claxton, G. (2000) 'Integrity and uncertainty – why young people need doubtful teachers', in C. Watkins, C. Lodge and R. Best (eds), *Tomorrow's Schools – Towards Integrity*. London: Routledge Falmer.

Cohen, S. (1989) 'Every school a clinic: a historical perspective on modern American education', in S. Cohen and L.C. Solomon, *From the Campus: Perspectives on the School Reform Movement*. London: Praeger.

Cooper, P. and McIntyre, D. (1996) *Effective Teaching and Learning: Teachers' and Students' Perspectives*. Buckingham: Open University Press.

Crace, J. (2000) 'Mind games', *Guardian*, 14 March:2.

Crook, C. (1994) *Computers and the Collaborative Experience of Learning*. London: Routledge.

Cuban, L. (1993) 'Computers meet classroom: classroom wins', *Teachers College Record*, 95 (2): 185–210.

Curtis, P. (2000) 'Teaching and learning in classrooms'. Unpublished assignment for MA in Education, Institute of Education, University of London.

Dagley, V. (2000) Private correspondance based on research for an Education Doctorate Degree, University of East Anglia (unpublished).

Day, C. (1991) 'Roles and relationships in qualitative research on teachers' thinking: a reconsideration', *Teaching and Teacher Education*, 7(5/6): 537–47.

Damon, W. and Phelps, E. (1989) 'Critical distinction among three approaches to peer education', *International Journal of Educational Research*, 13: 9–19.

Dennison, B. and Kirk, R. (1990) *Do, Review, Learn, Apply: A Simple Guide to Experiential Learning*. Oxford: Blackwell.

Department for Education and Employment (DfEE) (1998) *The Learning Age: A renaissance for a New Britain*. London: The Stationery Office.

Department of Education and Science (DES) (1989) *Discipline in Schools: Report of the Committee of Enquiry Chaired by Lord Elton*. London: HMSO.

Doyle, W. (1986) 'Classroom organization and management', in M.C. Wittrock (ed.), *Handbook of Research on Teaching*. 3rd edn. New York: Macmillan.

Dweck, C.S. (1986) 'Motivational practices affecting learning', *American Psychologist*, 41(10): 1040–8.

Dweck, C.S. (2000) *Self Theories: Their Role in Motivation, Personality, and Development*. Hove: Psychology Press.

Eraut, M., Alderton, J., Cole, G. and Senker, P. (1998) *Development of Knowledge and Skills in Employment*. Final report of a research project funded by The Learning Society Programme of the Economic and Social Research Council, University of Sussex, Institute of Education.

Ertmer, P.A. and Newby, T.J. (1996) 'The expert learner: strategic, self-regulated, and reflective', *Instructional Science*, 24 (1): 1–24.

Forret, M. (1998) 'Learning electronics: an accessible introduction'. Unpublished D.Phil. thesis, University of Waikato, New Zealand.

Fraser, A. (1999) 'Pupils' perceptions of a system of individual academic tutoring at key stage 4 and its effects: one school's experience'. Unpublished MA Dissertation, Institute of Education, University of London.

Freire, P. (1970) *Pedagogy of the Oppressed.* (trans. M.B. Ramos.) London: Penguin Books.

Gardner, H. (1983) *Frames of Mind: The Theory of Multiple Intelligencies,* New York: Basic Books.

Gardner, H. (1991) *The Unschooled Mind: How Children Think and How Schools Should Teach.* New York: Basic Books.

Gold, A. and Evans, J. (1998) *Reflecting on School Management.* London: Falmer Press.

Gillham, B. (1978) *Reconstructing Educational Psychology.* London: Croom Helm.

Gipps, C. (1995) *Beyond Testing: towards a theory of assessment.* London: The Falmer Press.

Gray, J., Hopkins, D., Reynolds, D., Wilcox, B., Farrell, S. and Jesson, D. (1999) *Improving Schools: Performance and Potential.* Buckingham: Open University Press.

Griffiths, P. (1995) 'Guidance and tutoring', in R. Best, P. Lang, C. Lodge and C. Watkins (eds), *Pastoral Care and Personal-Social Education: Entitlement and Provision.* London: Cassell.

Guardian (1999) 'Star performers . . . the most improved schools in England', *Guardian Results,* 25 November:8.

Hamblin, D. (1978) *Teachers and Pastoral Care.* Oxford: Blackwell.

Hannon, P. (1993) 'Conditions of learning at home and in school', in R. Merttens, D. Mayers, A. Brown and J. Vass (eds), *Ruling the Margins: Problematizing Parental Involvement.* London: IMPACT Project.

Hargreaves, D. (1991) 'Coherence and manageability: reflection on the National Curriculum and cross-curricular provision', *Curriculum Journal,* 2 (1): 33–41.

Hargreaves, D. (1995) *Mosaic of Learning: Schools and Teachers for the Next Century.* London: Demos.

Harris, S., Wallace, G. and Rudduck, J. (1995) '"It's not that I haven't learned much. It's just that I don't really understand what I'm doing": metacognition and secondary-school students', *Research Papers in Education,* 10 (2): 253–71.

Harrison, B. (1998) 'Managing pastoral care in schools: taking responsibility for people', in M. Calvert and J. Henderson (eds), *Managing Pastoral Care.* London: Cassell.

Hayes, C., Fonda, N. and Hillman, J. (1995) *Learning in the New Millennium.* London: National Commission on Education Briefing, New Series 5.

Head, K. and Taylor, P. (1997) *Readings in Teacher Development.* Oxford: Heinemann.

Honey, P. and Mumford, A. (1986) *The Manual of Learning Styles.* Maidenhead: Peter Honey.

Hughes, M. (1997) *Lessons Are for Learning.* Stafford: Network Educational Press.

International Commission on Education for the Twenty-First Century (ICE) (1996) *Learning: The Treasure Within.* Report to UNESCO of the Commission, chaired by Jacques Delors. Paris: UNESCO.

Keys, W. and Fernandes, C. (1993) *What do Students Think about School? Research into the Future with Positive and Negative Attitudes towards School and Education.* A report for the National Commission on Education. London: National Commission on Education.

Kitteringham, J. (1987) 'Pupils' perceptions of the role of the form tutor', *Pastoral Care in Education,* 5 (3): 206–17.

Kolb, D.A. (1984) 'Experiential learning', in M. Thorpe, R. Edwards and A. Hanson (eds), *Culture and Process of Adult Learning.* London: Routledge in association with the Open University.

Kruse, S.D., Louis, K.S. and Bryk, A.S. (1995) 'An emerging framework for analyzing school-based professional community', in K.S. Louis, S.D. Kruse and Associates (eds), *Professionalism and Community: Perspectives on Reforming Urban Schools.* Thousand Oaks, CA: Corwin Press.

Lieberman, A. and Miller, L. (2000) 'Teaching and teacher development: a new synthesis for a new century', in R.S. Brandt (ed.), *Education in a New Era*. Alexandria, V: ASCD.

Little, J.W. (1990) 'The persistence of privacy: autonomy and initiative in teachers' professional relationships', *Teachers College Record*, 91 (4): 509–36.

Lodge, C. (1995) 'School management for pastoral care and PSE', in R. Best, P. Lang, C. Lodge and C. Watkins (eds), *Pastoral Care and Personal-Social Education: Entitlement and Provision*. London: Cassell.

Lodge, C. (1997) 'What do children know, understand and articulate about effective learning?'. Unpublished EdD assignment, Institute of Education, University of London.

Lodge, C. (1999) 'From head of year to year curriculum coordinator and back again?', *Pastoral Care in Education*, 17 (4): 11–16.

Lodge, C. (2000a) 'Tutors and students' learning or why do schools have tutors?', *Pastoral Care in Education*, 18 (2): 35–41.

Lodge, C. (2000b) Unpublished research into effectiveness issues in one school.

Lodge, C. (2001) Unpublished research for EdD thesis at the University of London.

MacBeath, J. (1999) *Schools Must Speak for Themselves: The Case for School Self-Evaluation*. London: Routledge Falmer.

MacBeath, J. (2000) 'Schools for communities', in C. Watkins, C. Lodge and R. Best (eds), *Tomorrow's Schools – Towards Integrity*. London: Routledge Falmer.

MacBeath, J. and Myers, K. (1999) *Effective School Leaders*. London: Prentice-Hall.

MacDonald, J. (2000) 'Student views on careers education and guidance – what sort of feedback to careers co-ordinators?', in S. Askew (ed.), *Feedback for Learning*. London: Routledge Falmer.

Mann, C. (1995) 'Developing children's self-esteem through thinking skills in a supportive group setting'. Unpublished MEd Dissertation, University of Bristol.

Marland, M. and Rogers, R. (1997) *The Art of the Tutor: Developing your Role in the Secondary School*. London: David Fulton.

Marton, F., Dall'Allba, G. and Beaty, E. (1993) 'Conceptions of learning', *International Journal of Educational Research*, 19 (3): 277–300.

McIntyre, D. (1999) 'Has classroom teaching served its day?' Unpublished paper presented at Cambridge University School of Education, Research Seminar Series.

McLean, P. (2001) 'Perceptions of the impact of meditation on learning', *Pastoral Care in Education*, 19 (1): 31–5.

McMahon, T. (1999) 'Is reflective practice synonymous with action research?', *Educational Action Research*, 7 (1): 163–8.

McNamee, S. and Gergen, K. (eds) (1999) *Relational Responsibilities: Resources for Sustainable Dialogue*. Thousand Oaks, CA: Sage.

McNeil, L. (1986) *Contradictions of Control: School Structure and School Knowledge*. New York: Routledge and Kegan Paul.

Megahy, T. (1998) 'Managing the curriculum: pastoral care as a vehicle for raising student achievement', in M. Calvert and J. Henderson (eds), *Managing Pastoral Care*. London: Cassell.

Mitchell, C. and Sankey, L. (2000) *Profound Improvement: Building Capacity for a Learning Community*. Lisse: Swets and Zeitlinger.

Morgan, C. and Morris, G. (1999) *Good Teaching and Learning: Pupils and Teachers Speak*. Buckingham: Open University Press.

Mosely, J. and Tew, M. (1999) *Quality Circle Time in the Secondary Schools: a Handbook of Good Practice*. London: David Fulton.

Munro, J. (1999) 'Learning more about learning improves teacher effectiveness', *School Effectiveness and School Improvement,* 10 (2): 151–71.

National Association for Pastoral Care in Education(NAPCE) National Executive (1999) 'Pastoral leader standards', *Pastoral Care in Education,* 17 (4): 40–1.

Nisbet, J. and Shucksmith, J. (1984) *The Seventh Sense,* Scottish Council for Research in Education and Scottish Education Research Association, annual lecture.

O'Connor, J. and McDermott, I. (1997) *The Art of Systems Thinking: Essential Skills for Creativity and Problem Solving.* London: Thorsons.

OFSTED Report (1998) Report on Cheddar First School, Ref 123717. London: OFSTED.

OFSTED Report (1999) Report on Rooks Heath School, Ref 102240. London: OFSTED.

Pole, C. (1993) *Assessing and Recording Achievement: Implementing a New Approach in Schools.* Buckingham: Open University Press.

Reed, J. and Stoll, L. (2000) 'Promoting organisational learning in schools – the role of feedback', in S. Askew (ed.), *Feedback for Learning.* London: Routledge Falmer.

Resnick, L.B. (1987) 'Learning in school and out', *Educational Researcher,* 16 (99): 13–40.

Reynolds, K. (1995) 'The role of the form tutor: some research findings', *Pastoral Care in Education,* 13 (3): 29–33.

Rosenholtz, S. (1991) *Teachers' Workplace: The Social Organization of Schools.* New York: Longman.

Rudduck, J. (1991a) *Innovation and Change.* Milton Keynes: Open University Press.

Rudduck, J. (1991b) 'It's not labour and it's not play: teaching and learning in Secondary Schools', *Curriculum Journal,* 2 (2): 125–35.

Rudduck, J., Chaplain, R. and Wallace, G. (1996) *School Improvement: What Can Pupils Tell Us?* London: David Fulton.

Saljo, R. (1979) *Learning in the Learner's Perspective.* Gothenburg: Institute of Education, University of Gothenburg.

Salmon, P. (1998) *Life at School.* London: Constable.

Sandford, B. (1988) 'Writing reflectively', *Language Arts,* 65 (7): 652–7.

Schools Curriculum and Assessment Authority (SCAA) (1995) *Spiritual and Moral Development.* (Discussion Papers, 3.) London: SCAA.

Senge, P. (1990) *The Fifth Discipline: The Art and Practice of the Learning Organization.* London: Century Business.

Sizer, T. (1985) 'Common sense', *Educational Leadership,* 42 (6): 21–2.

Sockett, H. (1996) 'Teachers for the 21st century: redefining professional development', *National Association of Secondary School Principals Bulletin,* 80 (580): 22–9.

Smith, A. (1996) *Accelerated Learning in the Classroom.* Stafford: Network Educational Press.

Smith, R. (1993) 'Potentials for empowerment in critical educational research', *Australian Educational Researcher,* 20 (2): 75–93.

Stenhouse, L. (1975) *An Introduction to Curriculum Research and Development.* London: Heinemann.

Stoll, L. (1999) 'Developing schools' capacity for lasting improvement', *Improving Schools,* 2 (3): 32–9.

Stoll, L. and Smith, I. (1997) 'Closing the gap: what teachers expect and what they get'. Paper presented at the Tenth International Congress for School Effectiveness and Improvement, Memphis, Tennessee.

Sullivan, J. (2000) 'Stand and deliver – the teacher's integrity', in C. Watkins, C. Lodge and R. Best (eds), *Tomorrow's Schools – Towards Integrity.* London: Routledge Falmer.

Todd, E.S. and Higgins, S. (1998) 'Powerlessness in professional and parent partnerships', *British Journal of Sociology of Education*, 19 (2): 227–36.

Ulich, D., Jick, T. and Von Glinow, M.A. (1994) 'High impact learning: building and diffusing learning capability', in D. Bohi (ed.), *The Learning Organization in Action*. New York: American Management Association.

University of Bristol (2000) *The LEARN Project. Guidance for Schools on Assessment for Learning, CLIO Centre for Assessment Studies*. Website: www.qca.org.uk

Wallace, G. (1996) 'Engaging with learning', in J. Rudduck, R. Chaplain and G. Wallace (eds), *School Improvement: What Can Pupils Tell Us?* London: David Fulton.

Watkins, C. (1995) *Classrooms: Their Nature, Teachers' Knowledge Use and Some Implications for Improvement*, School Improvement Network, 6, March, 'Making a Difference in the Classroom'.

Watkins, C. (1999) 'The case for restructuring the UK secondary school', *Pastoral Care in Education*, 17 (4): 3–10.

Watkins, C. (2000) 'Feedback between teachers', in S. Askew (ed.), *Feedback for Learning*. London: Routledge Falmer.

Watkins, C. (2001) *Learning about Learning Enhances Performance*. National School Improvement Network Research Matters No 13. London: University of London, Institute of Education.

Watkins, C. and Butcher, J. (1995) *Individual Action Planning: Getting More from Learning*. London: London East Training and Enterprise Council, Cityside House, 40 Adler Street, London E1 1EE.

Watkins, C., Carnell, E., Lodge, C. and Whalley, C. (1996) *Effective Learning*. School Improvement Network Research Matters No 5. London: University of London, Institute of Education.

Watkins, C., Carnell, E., Lodge, C., Wagner, P. and Whalley, C. (2000) *Learning about Learning: Resources for Supporting Effective Learning*. London: Routledge Falmer.

Watkins, C. Lodge, C and Best, R. (eds), (2000) *Tomorrow's Schools – Towards Integrity*. London: RoutledgeFalmer.

Watkins, C. and Mortimore, P. (1999) 'Pedagogy: what do we know?', in P. Mortimore (ed.), *Understanding Pedagogy and its Impact on Learning*. London: Paul Chapman.

Watkins, C. and Wagner, P. (2000) *Improving School Behaviour*. London: Paul Chapman.

Wehlage, G.G., Rutter, R.A., Gregory, A., Smith, N.L. and Fernandez, R.R. (1989) *Reducing the Risk: Schools as Communities of Support*. Lewes: Falmer Press.

Wolfendale, S. (1992) *Empowering Parents and Teachers: Working for Children*. London: Cassell.

Author Index

Subject Index